SOCIAL
AND
CAMP-MEETING
SONGS,
FOR
THE PIOUS.

"While I live I will praise the Lord."—*Psalm* cxlvi. 2.

FOURTH EDITION.

BALTIMORE.

PUBLISHED BY ARMSTRONG & PLASKITT,

No 134, *Market-street.*

R. J. Matchett, printer.

1822.

DISTRICT OF MARYLAND—TO WIT:
BE IT REMEMBERED, That on the sixteenth day of April, in the forty-first year of the Independence of the United States of America, JOHN J. HARROD, of the said district, hath deposited in this office, the title of a book, the right whereof he claims as proprietor, in the words following, to wit:—

"Social and Camp-Meeting Songs, for the Pious. While I live I will praise the Lord———Psalm cxlvi. 2."

In conformity to the act of the Congress of the United States, entitled "An act for the encouragement of learning, by securing the copies of maps, charts, and books, to the authors and proprietors of such copies during the times therein mentioned;" and also to an act, entitled 'An act supplementary to an act, entitled "An act for the encouragement of learning by securing the copies of maps, charts, and books to the authors and proprietors of such copies, during the times therein mentioned;' and extending the benefits thereof to the arts of designing, engraving, and etching historical and other prints."

PHILIP MOORE,
Clerk of the District of Maryland.

New facsimile edition designed and edited by Kevin I. Slaughter
"Introduction..." and "Appendix" © copyright 2025, Kevin I. Slaughter

Hollow Square Books
BALTIMORE, JULY 2025
978-1-943687-38-1

Introduction to the Facsimile Edition

At the height of America's Second Great Awakening, *Social and Camp-Meeting Songs, for the Pious* emerged from Baltimore as a modest but potent devotional companion for an evangelical public on fire with religious zeal. First compiled by Methodist publisher and reformer John J. Harrod, with some editions published by Armstrong & Plaskitt. It was one of many hymnals publised over several decades by the two concerns. From this vantage, it is unclear the reasons for the path the book took being published under different names and with so many editions. The 1822 fourth edition—reprinted here in facsimile—stands as a fascinating artifact of American religious folk culture, situated at the convergence of Methodist enthusiasm, frontier piety, and the developing oral traditions that would later find their fullest musical expression in the shape-note movement that remains vibrant and alive today.

George Pullen Jackson, in *A Short History of American Religious Folk Song* (Hollow Square Books, 2025), underscored how early dissenters in America—Baptists, Methodists, Freewillers, and other grassroots sects—responded to the newfound religious liberty of the post-Revolutionary period by improvising new forms of worship: less refined, more ecstatic, and almost entirely popular in origin. This hymnal, first printed in the wake of those transformative decades, exemplifies that shift. It was designed for "the pious," certainly—but more to the point, for the *gathered*, the *converted*, and the *convicted*. These were not hymns to be read silently or contemplated in still pews—they were meant to be sung *aloud*, on the campgrounds, in homes, and in fervent prayer meetings.

Social and Camp-Meeting Songs includes no musical notation, as was common in this transitionary time. Its inclusion of now-familiar titles such as "Brethren, We Have Met to Worship"—which first appeared in print in the 1817 first edition of this very book—demonstrates its key role in shaping American hymnody. Authored by George Atkins and printed only a year after his death, this text later found its enduring musical home with the tune "Holy Manna" (by William Moore), a pairing first published in *The Southern Harmony* (1835), page 103. It entered *The Sacred Harp* in 1844 and appears today under the same name as song number 59, a staple of shape-note singings across traditions.

Several other texts found in Harrod's compilation would go on to appear in prominent shape-note tunebooks:

"Come and taste along with me"—saw the greatest range of most of the poetry here, winding up in four tunebooks under four different titles. The reason, in part, is that first line represents poetry by both John Leland and Caleb Jarvis Taylor. Leland's poetry appeared in *The Southern Harmonry* ("105 Come and Taste With Me") and *The Valley Pocket Harmonist* ("222 Farabee"). Taylor's appears in *The Christian Harmony* ("319 Weary Pilgrim") and *The Valley Pocket Harmonist* ("298 Pilgrim's Consolation").

"Farewell, my dear brethren"—A parting song found in *The Southern Harmony* (both "34 Imandra New", and "344 The Christian's Farewell") and *The Sacred Harp* ("45t Imandra New"), often sung at the close of all-day singings.

"O when shall I see Jesus"—Another John Leland text has been incredibly popular and widely reprinted. Not only does it appear in five of the six shape-note tunebooks we highlight in this book, but it appears in four different tunes in the 1991 revision of *The Sacred Harp* ("106 Ecstasy," "410 Mutual Love," "319 Religion is a Fortune," and "84 The Morning Trumpet").

I have spent a good deal of time compiling an Appendix that matches the poetry found in this collection to popular shape-note tunebooks. Modern tools make it easier than it once would have been, but both the tools and my ability to use them are far from perfect. Nevertheless, I was able to match

At the feet of my Saviour I'll there count my treasure,
  Where sin, pain, and sorrow can reach me no more.
Be bold and courageous, and fear not the devil,
  Though he should speak of you all manner of evil,
For though Satan rages, yet Jesus engages
  To bring us all shouting to Canaan's bright shore.

3 Like ships on the ocean we're toss'd by commotion,
  But Christ is the pilot, and he's a sure guide:
If sick and afflicted, kind love has a lotion
  Which flows in abundance from Jesus's side.
Though Satan's wild whirlwinds like deluges roaring,
  And floods of temptation as hail are down pouring,
Though devils should haunt you, yet let them not daunt you,
  For Jesus rules over the wind and the tide.

4. I feel his love blazing, my spirits are raising,
  Had I angel's pinions, away would I go,
And see that bright city, and hear angels praising,
  And all the enjoyment of glory to know,

SOCIAL

AND

CAMP-MEETING SONGS.

HYMN 1. P. M.

1. YE children of Zion, who're aiming for glory,
Enlisted with Jesus to fight against hell,
New Canaan's bright borders are now just before you,
Though Jordan's proud billows its banks overswell.
Ten thousand have cross'd it, and are now in glory,
A shouting and telling the triumphant story;
And Jesus, our Saviour, will bring us all over,
In the land of sweet Canaan, for ever to dwell.

2. This makes my heart joyful, it fills me with pleasure,
That suff'ring and toiling will one day be o'er.

over 60 poems to many tunes across 6 tunebooks published in the South between as early as 1835 and recently as 2024.

Each of these hymns, first shared as poetry in small books like Harrod's, found fuller voice in the shape-note tradition, often through oral transmission before being harmonized and codified. Jackson reminds us that revival hymnody "did not begin or end on the campground," but saturated daily life. Hymns from Harrod's book did not require musical literacy—only conviction. These were pocket-book texts, often sung from memory, and carried from kitchen to chapel to clearing.

It is worth noting that the source copy used in preparing this facsimile contains a known error: pages 93–96 are misprinted in place of pages 81–84. In an effort to balance the presentation as a facsimile, but also present the historical text which is the most important element, I have removed the duplicated pages of the source and typeset the otherwise missing text based on a later edition.

I present this facsimile not merely to preserve a rare hymnal, but to give a new life to a vital part of the Sacred Harp tradition's literary genealogy. *Social and Camp-Meeting Songs* shows us where the words first landed—before the tunes that we know so well.

—Kevin I. Slaughter
Baltimore, April 30, 2025

To our great God and Father, that shines
throughout heaven,
   All glory from saints and from angels be
given;
My heart's all on fire, my Jesus draws
nigher,
   His love, like an ocean, all through me doth
flow.

5. His love so constrains me, this earth can't
contain me,
   My soul is so joyful, I'm fill'd with new
wine,
'Tis grace that supports me, and glory awaits
me,
   While beams from sweet heav'n all round
me doth shine.
Bright angels attend me where'er I am going,
   Sweet Jesus directs me, whatever I'm do-
ing;
A subject of wonder, on which angels pon-
der,
   That beggars are raised to a life so divine.

HYMN 2.

On the Passion.

1. Saw ye my Saviour! Saw ye my Saviour!
Saw ye my Saviour and God?

Oh! he died on Calvary, to atone for you and me,
And to purchase our pardon with blood.

2. He was extended! He was extended!
Shamefully nail'd to the cross;
Oh! he bow'd his head and died, thus my Lord was crucified,
To atone for a world that was lost.

3. Jesus hung bleeding! Jesus hung bleeding!
Three dreadful hours in pain;
Oh! the sun refus'd to shine, when his majesty divine,
Was derided, insulted and slain.

4. Darkness prevailed! darkness prevailed!
Darkness prevail'd o'er the land,
O! the solid rocks were rent thro' creation's vast extent,
When the Jews crucified the God man.

5. When it was finish'd, when it was finish'd,
And, the atonement was made,
He was taken by the great, and embalm'd in spices sweet,
And in a new sepulchre was laid.

6. Hail, mighty Saviour! hail, mighty Saviour!
Prince and the author of peace,
Oh! he burst the bands of death, and triumphant thro' the east,
He ascended to mansions of bliss.

7. Now interceding! now interceding!
   Pleading that sinners may live;
   Crying Father, I have died! O behold my
      hands and side,
To redeem them, I pray thee forgive.

8. I will forgive them, I will forgive them,
   If they'll repent and believe,
   Let them now return to me and be reconcil'd
      to thee,
   And salvation they all shall receive.

HYMN 3.

1 HOW happy every child of grace,
  The soul that's fill'd with joy and peace,
  That bears the fruits of righteousness,
      And kept by Jesu's power;
  Their trespasses are all forgiv'n,
  They antedate the joys of heaven,
      In rapturous lays,
      Shout the praise,
      Of Jesu's grace,
      To a lost race
  Of sinners brought to happiness,
  Through the atoning blood of Jesus.

2. Satan may tempt, and hell may rage,
   And all the powers of earth besiege,
   Their united strength at once engage,
      To pluck a soul from Jesus;

1 *

The faithful soul laughs them to scorn,
He's heaven bound and heaven born.
    He'll watch and pray
    Night and day,
    Fight his way,
    Win the day,
And all his enemies dismay,
Through the mighty name of Jesus.

3. O monster death, thy sting is drawn,
O boasting grave, no trophies won,
  The soul triumphs through grace alone,
    To see the face of Jesus:
At length it bids the world adieu,
With all its vanity and show,
    The soul it flies,
    Through the skies,
    To paradise,
    And join its voice
In rapturous lays of love and praise
To the blessed name of Jesus.

4. When Gabriel's awful trump shall sound,
  And rend the rocks, convulse the ground,
  And swear that time is at an end,
    Arise, and come to judgment;
See lightnings flash, and thunder roll,
This earth wrapt like a parchment scroll;
    Comets blaze,
    Sinners raise
    Dread amaze,
    And horror seize

The guilty sons of Adam's race,
Unsaved from sin by Jesus.

5. The Christian fill'd with rapturous joy,
'Midst flaming worlds, he mounts on high
To meet his Saviour in the sky,
    And see the face of Jesus;
The soul and body re-unite,
And fill'd with glory infinite,
    Blessed day,
    Christians say,
    Will you pray,
    That we may
All join that happy company,
To praise the name of Jesus.

HYMN 4. P. M.

1. YE sons of war I pray draw near
And list as generous volunteers,
Become our royal brothers here,
    I mean as valiant soldiers;
You'll enter into present pay,
And feasting live from day to day,
Turn right about and march away,
    And Jesus will support you.

2. Ye careless sons of Adam's race,
Who long have trod in folly's ways,
O turn about to Zion's face,
    And meet Apollyon's forces;

Gird on your sword and glittering shield,
And with your helmet take the field,
And fight your way, and never yield,
   And Jesus will support you.

3. The bounty you shall have in hand,
If you will list in Jesu's band,
Your captain in the front will stand
   And beat your foes before you;
Come throw your rebel weapons down,
And seek for honour and renown,
And you shall wear a starry crown,
   For Jesus will support you.

4. You long have been the slaves of sin,
With dire corruption deep within,
The Christian warfare now begin,
   And face Apollyon's forces;
The breast-plate take of righteousness,
Your feet be shod with gospel peace,
Be daily at the throne of grace,
   And Jesus will support you.

5. Desert the cause of heaven's foe,
Before you plunge in endless woe,
Now courage take, to Jesus go,
   And he will now receive you;
From sin and Satan you'll get free,
And happy seasons you shall see,
And gain the Christian's liberty,
   For Jesus will support you.

6. No more in Satan's ranks appear,
But to our banner pray draw near,
We'll win the day, you need not fear,
    Though earth and hell oppose us.
Our captain he is always brave,
And able still his men to save;
He conquered death, hell and the grave,
    And he will still support you.

7. Let not sinners you affright,
Although they rage and vent their spite,
Wear but the Christian's armour right,
    And none can stand before you.
Although your parents should oppose,
Your dearest friends become your foes,
Yet sweetly with the gospel close,
    And Jesus will support you.

8. And when the war is at an end,
Our captain still will be our friend,
We'll wing our way, and up ascend,
    To reign with him in glory.
Then all our tears be wip'd away,
Our night be turn'd to endless day,
And on our golden harps we'll play,
    The joyful song of heaven.

HYMN 5. P. M.

1. O JESUS, my Saviour, to thee I submit,
With love and thanksgiving, fall down at thy feet,

The sacrifice offer, my soul, flesh and blood,
To thee my Redeemer, my Lord, and my God.

2. I love thee, I love thee, I love thee, my Lord,
I love thee, my Saviour, I trust in thy word,
I love thee, I love thee, and that thou dost know,
But how much I love thee I never can show.

3. I'm happy, I'm happy, O wond'rous account,
My joys are immortal, I stand on the mount,
I gaze on my treasure, and long to be there,
With angels my kindred, and Jesus my dear.

4. O Jesus, my Saviour, in thee I am blest,
My life and my treasure, my joy and my rest,
Thy grace be my theme, and thy name be my song,
Thy love doth inspire both my heart and my tongue.

5. O who is like Jesus? he is Salem's bright king,
He smiles and he loves me, and learns me to sing;
I'll praise him, I'll praise him, with notes loud and shrill,
While rivers of pleasure my spirit doth fill.

HYMN 6.

1. FROM the regions of love, lo! an angel descended,
And told the strange news, how the babe was attended;

Go shepherds and visit the wonderful stranger,
See yonder bright star, there's your God in a manger.

CHORUS.

Hallelujah to the lamb, who has purchas'd our pardon,
We'll praise him again when we pass over Jordan.

2. Glad tidings I bring, unto you and each nation,
Glad tidings of joy, now behold your salvation;
Then suddenly multitudes rais'd their glad voices,
And shout hallelujahs, while heaven rejoices.
Chor. Hallelujah, &c.

3. Now glory to God in the highest is given,
All glory to God is re-echo'd in heaven;
Around the whole earth, let us tell the glad story,
And sing of his love, his salvation and glory.
Chor. Hallelujah, &c.

4. Enraptured I burn, with delight and desire,
Such love, so divine, sets my soul all on fire;
Around the bright throne hosannahs are ringing,
O when shall I join them, and ever be singing.
Chor. Hallelujah, &c.

5. O Jesus ride on, thy kingdom is glorious,
O'er sin, death, and hell, thou'lt make us victorious;
Thy banner unfurl, let the nations surrender,
And own thee their Saviour, their God, and defender.

Chor. Hallelujah, &c.

HYMN 7. P. M.

1. BRIGHT scenes of glory strike my sense,
And all my passions capture,
Eternal beauties round me shine,
Infusing warmest rapture.
I dive in pleasures, deep and full
In swelling waves of glory;
And feel my Saviour in my soul,
And groan to tell my story.

2. I feast on honey, milk and wine,
I drink perpetual sweetness;
Mount Zion's beauties round me shine,
While Christ unfolds his glory!
No mortal tongue can show my joys,
Nor can an angel tell them;
Ten thousand times surpassing all
Terrestrial worlds or emblems.

3. My captivated spirit flies,
Through shining worlds of beauty,
Dissolved in blushes, loud I cry,
Inpraises loud and mighty.

And here I'll sing and swell the strain,
  Of harmony delighted;
And with the millions learn the notes
  Of saints in Christ united.

4. The bliss that rolls through those above,
    Through those in glory seated,
  Which causes them loud songs to sing,
    Ten thousand times repeated:
  Dart through my soul in radiant flame,
    Constraining loudest praises:
  O'erwhelming all my powers with joy,
    While all within me blazes.

5. When earth and sea shall be no more,
    And all their glory perish,
  When sun and moon shall cease to shine,
    And stars at midnight languish,
  My joys refin'd shall higher shine,
    With heav'n's radiant glory,
  And tell through one eternal day,
    Love's all immortal story.

HYMN 8. P. M.

1. O HOW I have long'd for the coming of God,
  And sought him by praying and searching his word,
  With watching and fasting my soul was opprest,
  Nor would I give over till Jesus had blest.

2. The news of his mercy, at length did appear,
According to promise, he answered my prayer;
And glory is opened in floods on my soul,
Salvation, from Zion's beginning to roll.

3. The news of his mercy is spreading abroad,
And sinners come crying and weeping to God,
Their mourning and praying is heard very loud,
And thousands find pardon in Jesus's blood.

4. Here's more, my dear Saviour, who fall at thy feet,
Opprest by a burden enormously great;
O raise them, my Jesus, to tell of thy love,
And shout hallelujah like angels above.

5. I'll sing, and I'll shout, and I'll shout and I'll sing,
O God make the nations with praises to ring,
With loud acclamations of Jesus's love,
And carry us all to the city above.

6. We'll wait for his chariot, it seems to draw near,
O come my dear Saviour, let glory appear;
We long to be singing and shouting above,
With angels o'erwhelmed in Jesus's love.

HYMN 9.

1. ALMIGHTY love inspire my heart with pure desire,
Until the sacred fire my soul doth renew,

I love the blessed Jesus, on whom each angel
   gazes,
And symphony increases, above the etherial
   blue.

CHORUS.

O give him glory. O give him glory,
O give him glory, for glory is his own;
I will give him glory, I will give him glory,
I will give him glory, for glory is his own.

2. My tender hearted Jesus, thy love my soul
   amazes,
Who came from heav'n to save us, when lost
   and undone:
No angel could redeem us, no seraph could
   retrieve us,
No arm could relieve us, but Jesus alone.

3. In him I have believed, he has my soul retrieved,
From sin he has redeemed my soul that was
   dead,
And now I love my Saviour, for I am in his favour,
And hope with him for ever, the golden
   streets to tread.

4. Yet here awhile I stay, in hope of that glad
   day,
Till I'm call'd away to the mansions above,

There to enjoy the treasure of unconsuming pleasure,
And shout in highest measure, hallelujahs of love.
Chor. O give him glory, &c.

HYMN 10. P. M.

1. HOW lost was my condition
   'Till Jesus made me whole;
   There is but one physician
   Can cure a sin-sick soul:
   Next door to death he found me,
   And snatch'd me from the grave
   To tell to all around me
   His wond'rous power to save.

2. The worst of all diseases
   Is light, compared to sin,
   On every part it seizes,
   But rages most within:
   'Tis palsy, plague, and fever,
   And madness all combin'd,
   And none but a believer,
   The least relief can find.

3. From men great skill professing,
   I sought a cure to gain;
   But this prov'd more distressing,
   And added to my pain.

Some said that nothing ailed me,
 Some gave me up for lost;
Thus every refuge failed me,
 And all my hopes were cross'd.

4. At length this great physician,
 (How matchless is his grace,)
Accepted my petition,
 And undertook my case:
First gave me sight to view him,
 For sin mine eyes had seal'd;
Then bade me look unto him,
 I look'd, and I was heal'd.

5. A dying, risen Jesus,
 Seen by an eye of faith,
At once from danger frees us,
 And saves the soul from death.
Come, then, to this physician,
 His help he'll freely give,
He makes no hard condition,
 'Tis only look and live.

HYMN 11.

1. MERCY, O thou son of David!
 Thus blind Bartemus he pray'd,
Others by thy grace are saved,
 Now vouchsafe to me thy aid:
For his crying many chid him,
 But he pray'd the louder still,
'Till his gracious Saviour bid him,
 Come and ask me what you will

2 *

2. Money was not what he wanted,
　　Though by begging us'd to live,
But he ask'd, and Jesus granted,
　　Alms which none but he could give:
Lord, remove this grievous blindness,
　　Let mine eyes behold the day,
Straight he saw, and won by kindness,
　　Follow'd Jesus in the way.

3. Now methinks I hear him singing,
　　Publishing to all around:
Friends, is not my case amazing,
　　What a Saviour I have found!
O that all the blind but knew him,
　　And would be advis'd by me;
Sure if they would come unto him,
　　He would cause them all to see.

4. Now I freely leave my garments,
　　Follow Jesus in the way,
He will guide me by his counsel,
　　Lead me to eternal day;
There I shall behold my Saviour,
　　Spotless, innocent and pure,
There with him to reign for ever,
　　If I to the end endure.

HYMN 12. L. M.

COME, ye that love the Lord indeed,
Who are from sin and bondage freed,

Submit to all the ways of God,
And walk the narrow, happy road.

CHORUS,

We're all united heart and hand,
Join'd in one band completely;
We're marching through Immanuel's land
Where the waters flow most sweetly.

2 Great tribulation you shall meet,
But soon shall walk the golden street;
Though hell may rage and vent its spite,
Yet Christ will save his heart's delight.
Chor. We're all united, &c.

3. That happy day will soon appear,
When Gabriel's trumpet you shall hear
Sound through the earth, yea, down to hell,
And call the nations great and small.
Chor. We're all united, &c.

4. Behold the world in burning flames,
The trumpet louder still proclaims,
The world must hear and know her doom;
The separation day is come.
Chor. We're all united, &c.

5. Behold the righteous marching home,
And all the angels bid them come,
While Christ the judge, these words proclaims,
"Here come my saints, I own their names.
Chor. We're all united, &c.

6. "Ye everlasting gates fly wide;
   Make ready to receive my bride;
   Ye harps of heav'n now sound aloud,
   Here comes the purchase of my blood"
      Chor. We're all united, &c.

7. In grandeur see the royal line,
   In glittering robes the sun outshine;
   See saints and angels join in one,
   And march in splendour to the throne.
      Chor. We're all united, &c.

8. They stand and wonder and look on;
   They join in one eternal song,
   Their great Redeemer to admire,
   While raptures set their souls on fire.
      Chor. We're all united, &c.

HYMN 13.

1. HAIL! sov'reign love, that first began
   The scheme to rescue fallen man:
   Hail! matchless free, eternal grace,
   That gave my soul a hiding place.

2. Against the God that rules the sky
   I fought, with hands uplifted high,
   Despis'd the offers of his grace,
   Too proud to seek a hiding place.

3. Enwrapt in dark Egyptian night,
   Was fond of darkness more than light,
   Madly I ran the sinful race,
   Secure without a hiding place.

4. But lo! the eternal counsel ran,
"Almighty love arrest the man!"
I felt the arrows of distress,
And found I had no hiding place.

5. Vindictive justice stood in view,
To Sinai's fiery mount I flew,
Stern justice cry'd, with frowning face,
This mountain is no hiding place.

6. But lo! a heav'nly voice I heard,
And mercy for my soul appear'd;
She led me on a pleasant pace,
To Jesus Christ, my hiding place.

7. Should seven-fold storms of thunder roll,
And shake the globe from pole to pole,
No thunder-bolt shall daunt my face,
For Jesus is my hiding place.

8. On him Almighty vengeance fell,
That might have crush'd a world to hell;
He bore it for a sinful race,
And thus became their hiding place.

9. A few more rolling scenes at most,
Will land me safe on Zion's coast;
There I shall sing a song of grace,
Safe in my glorious hiding place.

HYMN 14.

1. STOP, poor sinner, stop and think,
    Before your farther go,
Can you sport upon the brink
    Of everlasting woe?
Hell beneath is gaping wide,
    Vengeance waits the dread command,
Soon will stop your sport and pride,
    And sink you with the damn'd.

CHORUS.

Then be entreated now to stop,
    For unless you warning take,
Ere you are aware, you'll drop
    Into a burning lake.

2. Say, have you an arm like God,
    That you his will oppose?
Fear you not that iron rod
    With which he breaks his foes?
Can you stand in that great day,
    When his judgment he'll proclaim;
And the earth shall melt away,
    Like wax before the flame?
            Then be entreated, &c.

3. Ghastly death will quickly come,
    And drag you to the bar;
Then to hear your awful doom,
    Will fill you with dispair.

All your sins will round you croud,
  Sins of a blood crimson die;
Each for vengeance cry aloud,
  And what will you reply?
    Then be entreated, &c.

4. Though your hearts be made of steel,
    Your forehead lin'd with brass,
  God at length will make you feel,
    He will not let you pass:
  Sinners, then in vain will call,
    (Though they now despise his grace;)
  Rocks and mountains on us fall,
    And hide us from his face.
      Then be entreated, &c.

5. But as yet there is a hope,
    You may his mercy know:
  Though his arm be lifted up,
    He still forbears the blow:
  It was for sinners Jesus died;
    Sinners he invites to come:
  None that come shall be denied—
    He says there still is room.
      For Jesu's sake, I pray you stop, &c

HYMN 15.

1. THE son of man they did betray,
  He was condemn'd and led away,
  Think, O my soul, on that dread day:
    Look on mount Calvary.

Behold him lamb-like led along,
Surrounded by a wicked throng,
Accused by each lying tongue.
And then the Lamb of God they hung
　　Upon the shameful tree.

2. 'Twas thus the glorious sufferer stood,
With hands and feet nail'd to the wood;
From every wound a stream of blood
　　Came flowing down amain.
His bitter groans all nature shook,
And at his voice the rocks were broke,
And sleeping saints their graves forsook,
While spiteful Jews around him mock'd,
　　And laughed at his pain.

3. Now hung between the earth and skies,
Behold! in agonies he dies;
O sinners! hear his mournful cries,
　　Come see his tort'ring pain.
The morning sun withdrew his light,
Blush'd, and refus'd to view the sight:
The azure clothed in robes of night,
All nature mourn'd and stood affright,
　　When Christ the Lord was slain.

4. Hark! men and angels, hear the son,
He cries for help, but O! there's none,
He treads the wine-press all alone,
　　His garments stained with blood

In lamentations hear him cry,
"Eloi, lama sabacthani!"
Though death may close his languid eyes,
He soon will mount the upper skies,
    The conq'ring Son of God.

5. The Jews and Romans in a band,
With hearts like steel around him stand,
And mocking, say, "Come save the land,
    Come try yourself to free."
A soldier pierc'd him when he died,
Then healing streams came from his side,
And thus my Lord was crucified;
Stern justice now is satisfied,
    Sinners, for you and me.

6. Behold! he mounts the throne of state,
He fills the mediatorial seat,
While millions bowing at his feet,
    With loud hosannahs tell:
Though he endured exquisite pains,
He lead the monster death in chains:
Ye seraphs raise your highest strains,
With music fill bright Eden's plains,
    He conquer'd death and hell.

7. 'Tis done! the dreadful debt is paid,
The great atonement now is made:
Sinners on him your guilt was laid,
    For you he spilt his blood:

For you his tender soul did move,
For you he left the courts above,
That you the length and breadth might prove,
And height and depth of perfect love,
　　In Christ your smiling God.

8. All glory be to God on high,
Who reigns enthron'd above the sky :
Who sent his son to bleed and die,
　　Glory to him be giv'n ;
While heav'n above his praise resounds,
O Zion sing—his grace abounds ;
I hope to shout eternal rounds,
In flaming love, that knows no bounds,
　　When swallow'd up in heav'n.

HYMN 16.

1. DON'T you see my Jesus coming ?
　　Don't you see him in yonder cloud ?
With ten thousand angels round him,
　　See how they do my Jesus crowd!

2. Don't you see his arms extended ?
　　Don't you hear his charming voice ?
Each loving heart beats high for glory,
　　Oh! my Jesus is my choice,

3. Don't you see the saints ascending?
　　Hear them shouting through the air ?
Jesus smiling, trumpets sounding,
　　Now his glory they shall share.

4. Don't you see the heav'ns open,
　And the saints in glory there?
Shouts of triumph bursting round you,
　Glory, glory, glory here!

5. Come backsliders, tho' you've pierc'd him,
　And have caus'd his church to mourn;
Yet you may regain free pardon,
　If you will to him return.

6. Now behold each loving spirit,
　Shout the praise of his dear name;
View the smiles of their dear Jesus,
　While his presence feeds the flame.

7. There we'll range the fields of pleasure,
　By our dear Redeemer's side:
Shouting glory, glory, glory,
　While eternal ages glide.

HYNM 17.

1. THROUGHOUT the Saviour's life we trace,
Nothing but shame and deep distress,
　No period else is seen;
'Till he a spotless victim fell,
Tasting, in soul, a painful hell,
　Caus'd by the creature's sin.

2. On the cold ground methinks I see
My Saviour kneel and pray for me;
　For this I him adore;

Seiz'd with a chilly sweat throughout,
Blood drops did force their passage out
   Through every opening pore.

3. The piercing thorns his temple bore,
His back with lashes all was tore,
   Till thou the bones might see;
Mocking, they push'd him here and there,
Marking his way with blood and tears,
   Press'd by the heavy tree.

4. Thus up the hill he painful came,
Round him they mocked and made their game,
   At length his cross they rear.
And can you see the mighty God,
Cry out beneath sin's heavy load,
   Without one thankful tear?

5. Thus veiled in humanity,
He dies in anguish on the tree;
   What tongue his grief can tell?
The shudd'ring rocks their heads recline,
The morning sun refus'd to shine,
   When the Redeemer fell.

6. Shout, brethren, shout, in songs divine,
He drank the gall to give us wine,
   To quench our parching thirst:
Seraphs advance your voices higher,
Bride of the Lamb unite the choir,
   And laud the precious Christ.

HYMN 18.

1. LISTED into the cause of sin.
   Why should a good be evil?
   Music, alas, too long has been
   Press'd to obey the devil:
   Drunken or lewd, or light the lay,
   Flows to the soul's undoing:
   Widens and strews with flowers the way,
   Down to our utter ruin.

2. Who on the part of God will rise?
   Innocent sounds recover;
   Fly on the prey, and seize the prize,
   Plunder the carnal lover;
   Strip him of ev'ry moving strain,
   Ev'ry melting measure;
   Music in virtue's cause retain,
   Rescue the holy pleasure.

3. Come, let us try if Jesu's love,
   Will not as well inspire us;
   This is the theme of those above,
   This upon earth shall fire us:
   Try if your hearts are tuned to sing;
   Is there a subject greater?
   Harmony all its strains may bring,
   Jesus's name is sweeter.

4. Jesus the soul of music is,
   His is the noblest passion;
   Jesus's name is life and peace,
   Happiness and salvation.

Jesus's name the dead can raise,
   Show us our sins forgiven:
Fill us with all the life of grace,
   Carry us up to heaven.

5. Who have a right like us to sing?
      Us whom his mercy raises?
   Cheerful our hearts for Christ is king,
      Joyful are all our faces.
   Who of his perfect love partakes,
      He ever more rejoices:
   Melody in our hearts we make,
      Melody with our voices

6. He that a sprinkled conscience hath,
      He that in God is merry,
   Let him sing psalms the Spirit saith,
      Joyful and never weary;
   Offer the sacrifice of praise,
      In spirit never ceasing;
   Spiritual songs and anthems raise,
      Worship and thanks and blessing.

7. Then let us in his praises join
      Triumph in his salvation;
   Glory ascribe to love divine,
      Worship and adoration.
   Heaven already is begun,
      Open'd in each believer;
   Only believe, and then sing on,
      Heaven is ours for ever.

HYMN 19. P. M.

1. JESUS, at thy command,
    I launch into the deep,
And leave my native land,
    Where sin lulls all asleep:
For thee I would the world resign,
And sail to heaven with thee and thine.

2. Thou art my pilot—wise,
    My compass is thy word:
My soul each storm defies,
    While I have such a Lord:
I'll trust thy faithfulness and power,
To save me in the trying hour.

3. Though rocks and quicksands deep,
    Through all my passage lie,
Yet Christ will safely keep,
    And guard me with his eye:
My anchor, hope, will firm abide,
And ev'ry boisterous storm outride.

4. Whene'er becalm'd I lie,
    And storms forbear to toss,
Be thou, dear Lord, still nigh,
    Lest I should suffer loss:
For more the treach'rous calm I dread
Than tempests bursting o'er my head.

5. By faith I see the land,
    The port of endless rest;

My soul, thy sails expand,
 And fly to Jesu's breast:
O may I gain the heavenly shore,
Where winds and waves disturb no more.

6. Come, Holy Ghost, and blow
 A prosperous gale of grace:
Waft me from all below,
 To heaven my destin'd place:
There in full sail, my port I'll find,
And leave the world and sin behind.

HYMN 20.

1. THE voice of free grace
 Cries escape to the mountain,
For Adam's lost race,
 Christ hath open'd a fountain:
For sin and transgression
 And ev'ry pollution,
His blood flows most freely
 In sreams of ablution.

CHORUS.

Hallelujah to the Lamb
 Who has purchas'd our pardon;
We will praise him again
 When we pass over Jordan.

2. That fountain so clear,
 In which all may find pardon,
From Jesus's side
 Flows plenteous redemption:

Though your sins were increased
  As high as a mountain,
His blood it flows freely:
  O come to this fountain.
       Hallelujah, &c.

3. Blest Jesus ride on,
    Thy kingdom is glorious,
  O'er sin, death, and hell,
    Thou wilt make us victorious.
  Thy name shall be prais'd
    In the great congregation,
  And saints shall delight
    In ascribing salvation.
       Hallelujah, &c.

4. When on Zion we stand,
    Having gain'd the blest shore,
  With our harps in our hands,
    We will praise him evermore;
  We'll range the bles' fields,
    On the banks of the river,
  And sing hallelujahs
    For ever and ever.
       Hallelujah, &c.

HYMN 21. P. M.

1. YE jewels of my master,
    Who shine with heavenly rays,
  Amid the beams of glory
    Reflect immortal blaze.

Ye diamonds of beauty,
   With pleasing lustre crown'd,
Of heavenly extraction,
   To Zion's city bound.

2. Ye lambs of my Redeemer,
   The purchase of his blood,
Who feed among the lilies,
   Beside the purple flood;
Go on, ye happy pilgrims,
   Your journey still pursue,
And at an humble distance
   I'll sing and follow too.

3. When I behold your order,
   And harmony of soul,
And heard divinest numbers
   In pure devotion roll,
And gems immortal glowing
   With such enlivening grace,
I view'd the Saviour's image
   Imprest on every face.

4. Speak often to each other,
   To cheer the fainting mind,
And often be your voices
   In pure devotion join'd;
Though trials may await you,
   The crown before you lies;
Take courage, brother pilgrims,
   And soon you'll win the prize.

Though your sins were increased
    As high as a mountain,
His blood it flows freely:
    O come to this fountain.
            Hallelujah, &c.

3. Blest Jesus ride on,
    Thy kingdom is glorious,
O'er sin, death, and hell,
    Thou wilt make us victorious.
Thy name shall be prais'd
    In the great congregation,
And saints shall delight
    In ascribing salvation.
            Hallelujah, &c.

4. When on Zion we stand,
    Having gain'd the blest shore,
With our harps in our hands,
    We will praise him evermore;
We'll range the bles' fields,
    On the banks of the river,
And sing hallelujahs
    For ever and ever.
            Hallelujah, &c.

HYMN 21. P. M.

1. YE jewels of my master,
    Who shine with heavenly rays,
Amid the beams of glory
    Reflect immortal blaze.

Ye diamonds of beauty,
  With pleasing lustre crown'd,
Of heavenly extraction,
  To Zion's city bound.

2. Ye lambs of my Redeemer,
  The purchase of his blood,
Who feed among the lilies,
  Beside the purple flood;
Go on, ye happy pilgrims,
  Your journey still pursue,
And at an humble distance
  I'll sing and follow too.

3. When I behold your order,
  And harmony of soul,
And heard divinest numbers
  In pure devotion roll,
And gems immortal glowing
  With such enlivening grace,
I view'd the Saviour's image
  Imprest on every face.

4. Speak often to each other,
  To cheer the fainting mind,
And often be your voices
  In pure devotion join'd;
Though trials may await you,
  The crown before you lies;
Take courage, brother pilgrims,
  And soon you'll win the prize.

5. Ye shall be mine, says Jesus,
   In that auspicious day,
When I make up my jewels,
   Releas'd from cumberous clay.
He'll polish and refine you
   From worthless dross and tin,
And to this heavenly kingdom
   Will bid you enter in.

6. On that important morning,
   When bursting thunders sound,
And nimble light'nings waving,
   Shall wing the gloom profound,
Lift up your heads rejoicing,
   And clap your joyful hands,
Lo! you're redeem'd for ever
   From death's corrupted bands.

7. As Aaron, with his girdle
   In shining jewels drest,
Bore all the tribes of Israel
   Inscrib'd upon his breast,
So will the priests of Zion,
   Before the Father's throne
Present the heirs of glory,
   And God their kindred own.

8. The golden bells will echo
   Around the sacred hill;
And sweet immortal anthems,
   The vocal regions fill;

In everlasting beauty
  The shining millions stand,
Safe on the Rock of Ages,
  Amid the promis'd land.

9 We'll range the wide dominion
  Of our Redeemer round,
And in dissolving raptures
  Be lost in love profound:
While all the flaming harpers
  Begin the lasting song,
With hallelujahs rolling
  From the unnumber'd throng.

HYMN 22. P. M.

1. BURST, ye emerald gates, and bring
    To my raptur'd vision,
All the ecstatic joys that spring
    Round the bright Elysian:
Lo! we lift our longing eyes,
Break, ye intervening skies;
Sons of righteousness, arise,
Ope the gates of Paradise.

2. Floods of everlasting light,
    Freely flash before him:
Myriads with supreme delight,
    Instantly adore him;
Angelic trumps resound his fame,
Lutes of lucid gold proclaim
All the music of his name;
Heaven echoing the theme.

3. Four and twenty elders rise
   From their princely station;
Shout his glorious victories,
   Sing the great salvation;
Cast their crowns before his throne,
Cry in reverential tone,
Glory be to God alone,
Holy! Holy! Holy One!

4. Hark! the thrilling symphonies,
   Seem, methinks, to seize us;
Join we to the holy lays—
   Jesus—Jesus—Jesus!
Sweetest sound in seraph's song,
Sweetest note on mortal's tongue,
Sweetest carol ever sung—
Jesus—Jesus flow along.

HYMN 23. P. M.

1. COME and taste along with me,
   Consolation running free;
   From my Father's wealthy throne,
   Sweeter than the honey comb.

2. Why should Christians feast alone,
   Two are better far than one,
   The more that come with free good will,
   Makes the banquet sweeter still.

3. Now I go to heaven's door,
Asking for a little more,
Jesus gives a double share,
Calling me his chosen heir.

4 Goodness running like a stream,
Through the new Jerusalem;
By its constant breaking forth,
Sweetens earth and heaven both.

5. Saints in glory sing aloud,
When they see an heir of God,
Coming in at heaven's door,
Making up the numbers more.

6. Heav'n here, and heav'n there,
Comforts flowing every where,
This I boldly can attest,
That my soul has got a taste.

7. Now I go rejoicing home,
From the banquet of perfume;
Gleaning manna on the road,
Dropping from the mount of God.

HYMN 24. L. M.

1. OH! give me, Lord, my sins to mourn,
My sins which have thy body torn;
Give me, with broken heart, to see
Thy last tremendous agony.

2. O could I gain the mountain's height,
And gaze upon the wond'rous sight:
O that with Salem's daughters, I
Could stand and see my Saviour die.

3. I'd hang around his feet, and cry,
Lord, save a soul condemn'd to die;
And let a wretch come near thy throne,
To plead the merits of thy Son.

4. Father of mercy, drop thy frown,
And give me shelter in thy Son;
And with my broken heart comply,
O give me Jesus or I die.

5. O Lord, deny me what thou wilt,
If thou wilt ease me of my guilt;
Good Lord, in mercy hear me cry
And give me Jesus or I die.

6. O save my soul from gaping hell,
Or else with devils I must dwell;
Oh, might I enter, now I'm come,
Lord Jesus save me or I'm gone.

HYMN 25. P. M.

1. O WHEN shall I see Jesus,
    And dwell with him above,
To drink the flowing fountains
    Of everlasting love?

When shall I be deliver'd,
  From this vain world of sin,
And with my blessed Jesus
  Drink endless pleasures in?

2. But now I am a soldier,
  My captain's gone before,
He's given me my orders,
  And tells me not to fear;
And if I hold out faithful,
  A crown of life he'll give,
And all his valiant soldiers
  Eternal life shall have.

3, Through grace, I am determin'd
  To conquer though I die,
And then away to Jesus,
  On wings of love I'll fly:
Farewell to sin and sorrow,
  I bid them all adieu,
And you my friends, prove faithful,
  And on your way pursue.

4 And if you meet with troubles,
  And trials on the way,
Then cast your care on Jesus,
  And don't forget to pray.
Gird on the heavenly armour
  Of faith, and hope, and love,
And when your race is ended
  You'll reign with him above.

5. O do not be discourag'd,
   For Jesus is your friend,
And if you lack for knowledge,
   He'll not refuse to lend:
Neither will he upbraid you,
   Though often you request;
He'll give you grace to conquer,
   And take you home to rest.

HYMN 26. P. M.

Description of Christ.

1. O THOU, in whose presence
      My soul takes delight,
   On whom in affliction I call;
      My comfort by day,
      And my song in the night,
   My hope, my salvation, my all.

2. Where dost thou at noon-tide
      Resort with thy sheep,
   To feed on the pastures of love?
      For why in the valley
      Of death should I weep,
   Or alone in the wilderness rove.

3. O why should I wander
      An alien from thee,
   And cry in the desert for bread:
      Thy foes will rejoice,
      When my sorrows they see,
   And smile at the tears I have shed.

4. Ye daughters of Zion,
Declare, have you seen
The star that on Israel shone?
Say if in your tents
My Beloved has been,
And where with his flocks he is gone?

5 This is my Beloved,
His form is divine,
His vestments shed odours around;
The locks on his head
Are as grapes on the vine,
When autumn with plenty is crown'd.

6 The roses of Sharon,
The lilies that grow,
In the vales, on the banks of the streams,
On his cheek in the beauty
Of excellence blow—
And his eyes are as quivers of beams

7 His voice, as the sound
Of the dulcimer sweet,
Is heard through the shadows of death;
The cedars of Lebanon
Bow at his feet,
The air is perfum'd with his breath.

8. His lips as a fountain
Of righteousness flow,
That waters the garden of grace,
From which their salvation
The Gentiles shall know,
And bask in the smiles of his face.

9. Love sits in his eye-lids,
    And scatters delight
Thro' all the bright mansions on high:
    Their faces the cherubims
    Veil in his sight,
And tremble with fulness of joy.

10. He looks, and ten thousand
    Of angels rejoice,
And myriads wait for his word;
    He speaks, and eternity
    Fill'd with his voice,
Re-echoes the praise of the Lord.

SECOND PART.

1. HIS vestments of righteousness
    Who shall describe!
Its purity, words would defile.
    The heav'ns from his presence
    Fresh beauties imbibe,
And earth is made rich by his smile.

2. Such is my Beloved,
    In excellence bright,
When pleas'd he looks down from above,
    Like the morn when he breathes
    From the chambers of light,
And comforts his people with love.

3. But when arm'd with vengeance,
    In terror he comes,
The nations rebellious to tame,

The reins of omnipotent
Power he assumes,
And rides in a chariot of flame.

4. A two-edged sword
From his mouth issues forth,
Bright quivers of fire are his eyes;
He speaks, and black tempests
Are seen in the north,
And storms from their caverns arise.

5. Ten thousand destructions,
That wait for his word,
And ride on the wings of his breath,
Fly swift as the wind
At the nod of their Lord,
And deal out the arrows of death.

6. His cloud-bursting thunders
Their voices resound,
Through all the vast regions on high;
'Till from the deep centre
Loud echoes rebound,
And meet the quick flame in the sky.

7. The portals of heav'n
At his bidding obey,
And expand ere his banner appear;
Earth trembles beneath,
'Till her mountains give way,
And hell shakes her fetters with fear.

8. When he treads on the clouds
As the dust of his feet,
And grasps the big storm in his hand

What eye the fierce glance
Of his anger shall meet,
Or who in his presence shall stand.

HYMN 27. L. M.

1 O GOD, my heart with love inflame,
That I may in thy holy name,
Aloud in songs of praise rejoice,
While I have breath to raise my voice;
Then I will shout, then I will sing,
And make the heavenly arches ring;
I'll sing and shout for evermore,
On that eternal, happy shore.

2. O hope of glory, Jesus, come!
And make my heart thy constant home;
For the small remnant of my days
I want to sing and shout thy praise.
O give me, Lord, a heart to pray,
And live rejoicing ev'ry day;
To give thee thanks in ev'ry thing,
And sing and shout, and shout and sing.

3. When on my dying bed I lie,
Lord, give me strength to shout and pray:
And praise thee with my latest breath,
Until my voice is lost in death.
Then, brethren, sisters, shouting come
My body follow to the tomb:
And as you march the solemn road,
Loud sing and shout the praise of God.

4 Then you below, and I above,
We'll shout and praise the God we love,
Until the great tremendous day,
When Gabriel's trump shall wake our clay;
Then from our dusty beds we'll spring,
And shout, O Death, where is thy sting!
O Grave, where is the victory!
We'll shout to all eternity.

5 Our race is run, we've gain'd the prize,
Then shall the sov'reign of the skies,
With smiles unto his children say,
Come reign with me in endless day
Then on that happy, happy shore,
We'll shout and sing our suff'rings o'er,
We'll sing and shout, and shout and sing,
And make the heavenly arches ring.

HYMN 28. L. M.

1. THIS life's a dream, an empty show,
But the bright world to which I go,
Hath joys substantial and sincere;
When shall I wake and find me there?

2. O glorious hour! O blest abode!
I shall be near, and like my God!
And flesh and sin no more control
The sacred pleasures of the soul.

3. My flesh shall slumber in the ground,
'Till the last trumpet's joyful sound:
Then burst the chains with sweet surprise,
And in my Saviour's image rise.

HYMN 29. C. M.

1. FROM all that's mortal, all that's vain
   And from this earthly clod,
  Arise, my soul, and strive to gain
   Some fellowship with God.

2. Say, what is there below the sky,
   Or all the paths thou'st trod,
  Can suit thy wishes or thy joys,
   Like fellowship with God?

3. Not life nor all the toys of art,
   Nor pleasure's flow'ry road,
  Can to my soul such bliss impart
   As fellowship with God.

4. Not health nor friendship here below,
   Nor wealth, that golden load,
  Can such delights and comforts show
   As fellowship with God.

5. When I in love am made to bear
   Affliction's needful rod,
  Light, sweet, and kind the strokes appear,
   Through fellowship with God.

6. In fierce temptation's fiery bla t,
   And dark distraction's road,
  I'm happy, if I can but taste
   Some fellowship with God

7. And when the icy arms of death,
   Shall chill my flowing blood,
 With joy I'll yield my latest breath
   In fellowship with God.

8. When I at last to heav'n ascend,
   And join that bless'd abode;
 There an eternity I'll spend
   In fellowship with God.

HYMN 30 P. M.

1. THERE is a land of pleasure,
    Where streams of joy for ever roll;
  'Tis there I have my treasure,
    And there I hope to rest my soul.
  Long darkness dwelt around me,
    With scarcely once a cheering ray:
  But since my Saviour found me,
    A light has shone along my way.

2. My way is full of danger,
    But it's the path that leads to God;
  Then, like a valiant soldier,
    I'll dauntless keep the happy road.
  Now I must gird my sword on,
    My helmlet, breastplate, and my shield,
  And fight the host of Satan,
    Until I gain the heav'nly field.

3. I'm on my way to Canaan,
    Still guarded by my Saviour's hand;
  O come along, dear sinner,
    And see Immanuel's happy land

To all that stay behind me,
  I bid a long, a long farewell!
O come, or you'll repent it,
  When you do reach the gates of hell.

4. The vale of tears surround me,
  And Jordan's current rolls before,
O how I stand and tremble
  To hear the dismal waters roar!
Whose hand shall then support me,
  And keep my soul from sinking there;
From sinking down to darkness,
  And to the regions of despair.

5 The waves shall not affright me,
  Although they're deeper than the grave,
If Jesus will stand by me,
  I'll calmly ride on Jordan's waves:
His word has calm'd the ocean,
  His lamp has cheer'd the gloomy vale:
O may this friend be with me,
  When through the gates of death I sail.

6 Then come, thou king of terror,
  And with thy weapons lay me low!
I soon shall reach that region,
  Where everlasting pleasures flow:
Now, Christians, I must leave you,
  A few more days to suffer here;
Through grace I soon shall meet you—
  My soul exults—I'm almost there.

7. Soon the archangel's trumpet
    Shall shake the globe from pole to pole,
And all the wheels of nature
    Shall in a moment cease to roll.
Then I shall see my Saviour,
    With shining ranks of angels come,
To execute his vengeance,
    And take his ransom'd people home.

HYMN 31. P. M.

1. JERUSALEM, my happy home,
    O how I long for thee!
When will my sorrows have an end?
    Thy joys when shall I see?

2. Thy walls are all of precious stone,
    Most glorious to behold;
Thy gates are richly set with pearl,
    Thy streets are pav'd with gold.

3. Thy garden and thy pleasant walks,
    My study long have been;
Such dazzling views by human sight,
    Has never yet been seen.

4. If heaven be thus glorious, Lord,
    Why should I stay from thence?
What folly's this that I should dread
    To die and go from hence?

5. Reach down, O Lord, thy arm of grace,
   And cause me to ascend,
Where congregations ne'er break up,
   And sabbaths never end.

6 Jesus, my Lord, to glory's gone,
   Him will I go and see;
And all my brethern here below,
   Will soon come after me.

7. My friends, I bid you all adieu,
   I leave you in God's care;
And if I never more see you,
   Go on, I'll meet you there.

8. When we've been there ten thousand years,
   Bright shining as the sun,
We've no less days to sing God's praise
   Than when we first begun.

HYMN 32. L. M.

1. FAREWELL, dear friends, I must be gone,
   I have no home or stay with you;
I'll take my staff and travel on,
   'Till I a better world do view;
          Farewell, farewell, farewell,
          My loving friends farewell.

2. Farewell, my friends, time rolls along,
   Nor waits for mortals, care or bliss,
I leave you here, and travel on,
   'Till I arrive where Jesus is.
          Farewell, &c.

3. Farewell, my brethren in the Lord,
   To you I'm bound in cords of love;
Yet we believe his gracious word,
   That soon we all shall meet above.
                    Farewell, &c.

4. Farewell, old soldiers of the cross,
   You've struggled long and hard for heav'n;
You've counted all things here but dross,
   Fight on, the crown shall soon be giv'n.
                    Farewell, &c.

5. Farewell, ye blooming sons of God,
   Sore conflicts yet await for you:
Yet dauntless keep the heav'nly road,
   'Till Canaan's happy land you view.
          Fight on, fight on, fight on,
          The crown shall soon be giv'n.

6. Farewell, poor careless sinners too,
   It grieves my heart to leave you here,
Eternal vengeance waits for you;
   O turn, and find salvation near.
          O turn, O turn, O turn,
          And find salvation near.

HYMN 33. P M.

1 THE Lord's into his garden come,
   The spices yield a rich perfume,
      The lilies grow and thrive;

Refreshing showers of grace divine,
From Jesus flow to every vine,
And makes the dead revive.

2. O that this dry and barren ground
In springs of water may abound,
A fruitful soil become;
The desert blossom as the rose,
When Jesus conquers all his foes
And makes his people one.

3. The glorious time is coming on,
The gracious work is now begun,
My soul a witness is;
I taste and see the pardon free
For all mankind as well as me;
Who come to Christ may live.

4. The worst of sinners here may find
A Saviour merciful and kind,
Who will them all receive;
None are too vile who will repent
Out of one sinner legions went,
The Lord did him relieve.

5. Come, brethren dear, who know the Lord,
And taste the sweetness of his word,
In Jesu's way go on:
Our troubles and our trials here,
Will only make us richer there,
When we arrive at home.

6. We feel that heav'n is now begun,
   It issues from the sparkling throne,
      From Jesu's throne on high:
   It comes in floods, we can't contain,
   We drink, and drink, and drink again,
      And yet we still are dry.

7. But when we come to dwell above,
   And all surround the throne of love,
      We'll drink a full supply:
   Jesus will lead his armies through,
   To living fountains where they flow,
      That never will run dry.

8. 'Tis there we'll reign, and shout, and sing,
   And make the upper regions ring,
      When all the saints get home:
   Come on, come on, my brethren dear,
   Soon we shall meet together there,
      For Jesus bids us come.

9. Amen, Amen, my soul replies,
   I'm bound to meet you in the skies,
      And claim my mansion there:
   Now here's my heart, and here's my hand,
   To meet you in that heav'nly land,
      Where we shall part no more.

HYMN 34. P M.

1. AWAK'D by Sina's awful sound,
   My soul in guilt and thrall I found,
      I knew not what to do;

O'erwhelm'd with guilt, and anguish slain,
The sinner must be born again,
   Or sink in endless woe.

2. Amaz'd I stood, but could not tell,
Which way to shun the gates of hell,
   For death and hell drew near;
I strove indeed, but strove in vain;
The sinner must be born again,
   Still sounded in my ear.

3. Then to the law I trembling fled,
It pour'd it curses on my head,
   I no relief could find:
This fearful truth I found remain,
The sinner must be born again
   O'erwhelm'd my troubled mind.

4. Again did Sina's thunder roll,
And guilt lay heavy on my soul,
   A vast unwieldy load:
Alas! I read and found it plain,
The sinner must be born again,
   Or drink the wrath of God.

5. The saints I heard with rapture tell
How Jesus conquer'd death and hell
   And broke the fowler's snare;
But when I found this truth remain,
The sinner must be born again,
   I sunk in deep despair.

6. While thus my soul in anguish lay,
Jesus of Naz'reth passed that way,
I felt his pity move:
The sinner by his justice slain,
Now by his grace is born again,
And sings redeeming love.

7. To heaven the joyful tidings flew.
The angels tuned their harps anew,
And loftier sounds did raise:
All hail the lamb that once was slain
Unnumber'd millions born again,
Shall shout thy endless praise.

HYMN 35. L. M.

The good old way.

1 LIFT up your hearts, Immanuel's friends,
And taste the pleasure Jesus sends;
Let nothing cause you to delay,
But hasten on the good old way.

CHORUS.

*And I'll sing hallelujah,
And glory be to God on high,
And I'll sing hallelujah,
There's glory beaming thro' the sky.*

2. Our conflicts here, though great they be,
Shall not prevent our victory;
If we but watch, and strive, and pray,
Like soldiers in the good old way.
     And I'll sing &c.

3. O good old way! how sweet thou art,
May none of us from thee depart,
But may our actions always say
We're marching in the good old way.
    And I'll sing, &c.

4. Though Satan may his powers employ,
Our happiness for to destroy,
Yet never fear, we'll gain the day,
And shout and sing the good old way.
    And I'll sing, &c.

5. And when on Pisgah's top we stand,
And view, by faith, the promis'd land,
Then we may sing, and shout, and pray,
And march along the good old way.
    And I'll sing, &c.

6. Ye valiant souls for heaven contend,
Remember glory's at the end;
Our God will wipe all tears away
When we have run the good old way.
    And I'll sing, &c.

7. Then far beyond this mortal shore,
We'll meet with those who've gone before,
And shout to think we've gain'd the day,
By marching in the good old way.
    And I'll sing, &c.

HYMN 36. P. M.

1. DARK and thorny is the desert
 Through which pilgrims make their way;

Yet beyond this vale of sorrow,
   Lie the fields of endless day;
Fiends loud howling through the desert
   Make them tremble as they go,
And the fiery darts of Satan
   Often bring their courage low.

2. O young soldiers, are you weary,
   Of the roughness of the way;
Does your strength begin to fail you,
   And your vigour to decay?
Jesus, Jesus, will go with you:
   He will lead you to his throne;
He who dy'd his garments for you,
   And the wine-press trod alone.

3. He whose thunder shakes creation,
   He who bids the planets roll:
He who rides upon the tempest,
   And whose sceptre sways the whole:
Round him are ten thousand angels,
   Ready to obey command,
They are always hov'ring round you,
   'Till you reach the heav'nly land.

4. There, on flow'ry hills of pleasure,
   Lie the fields of endless rest;
Love, and joy, and peace forever
   Reign and triumph in your breast.
Who can paint the scenes of glory
   Where the ransom'd dwell on high,
They on golden harps for ever
   Sound redemption through the sky!

5. There's a million of flaming seraphs
 Who fly across the heav'nly plain,
Where they sing immortal praises;
 Glory, glory. is their strain.
But methinks a sweeter concert,
 Makes the heav'nly arches ring:
And the song is heard in Zion,
 Which the angels cannot sing.

6. O their crowns! how bright they sparkle,
 Such as monarchs never wore;
They are gone to richer pastures,
 Jesus is their shepherd there.
Hail! ye happy, happy spirits,
 Death no more shall make you fear,
Grief nor sorrow, pain nor anguish,
 Shall no more distress you there.

HYMN 37. L. M.

1. JESUS! and shall it ever be
A mortal man asham'd of thee!
Asham'd of thee, whom angels praise,
Whose glories shine through endless days.

2. Asham'd of Jesus! sooner far
Let evening blush to own a star;
He sheds the beams of light divine
O'er this benighted soul of mine.

3. Asham'd of Jesus! just as soon
Let midnight be asham'd of noon;
'Tis midnight with my soul till he,
Bright Morning Star, bids darkness flee.

4. Asham'd of Jesus! that dear friend
On whom my hopes of heav'n depend!
No, when I blush—be this my shame
That I no more revere his name.

5. Asham'd of Jesus! yes, I may
When I've no guilt to wash away;
No tears to wipe, no good to crave,
No fears to quell, no soul to save.

6. 'Till then—nor is my boasting vain,
'Till then I boast a Saviour slain;
And O may this my glory be,
That Christ is not asham'd of me.

7 His institutions I will prize,
Take up my cross—the shame despise;
Dare to defend his noble cause,
And yield obedience to his laws.

HYMN 38. L. M.

1 THERE is a heav'n o'er yonder skies,
A heav'n where pleasure never dies,
A heav'n I sometimes hope to see,
But fear again it's not for me.
But Jesus, Jesus, is my friend, O hallelujah,
Hallelujah, Jesus, Jesus, is my friend.

2. the way is difficult and straight,
And narrow is the gospel gate;

Ten thousand dangers are therein,
Ten thousand snares to take me in.
But Jesus, &c.

3. I travel through a world of foes,
Through conflicts sore my spirit goes;
The tempter cries, I ne'er shall stand,
Nor reach fair Canaan's happy land.
But Jesus, &c.

4. The way of dangers I am in,
Beset with devils, men and sin;
But in this way thy track I see,
And mark'd with blood it seems to be.
Sweet Jesus. &c.

5. Come life, come death, come then what will,
His footsteps I will follow still;
Through dangers thick and hell's alarms,
I shall be safe in his dear arms,
O Jesus, &c.

6. Then, O my soul, arise and sing,
Yonder's thy Saviour, friend and king,
With pleasing smiles he now looks down,
And cries "press on, and here's the crown,
O Jesus, &c.

7. "Prove faithful then a few more days.
Fight the good fight and win the race,
And then thy soul with me shall reign,
Thy head a crown of glory gain,."
O Jesus, &c.

8. My flesh shall slumber in the ground,
'Till the last joyful trump shall sound,
Then burst the chains with sweet surprise,
And in my Saviour's image rise.
O Jesus, &c.

HYMN 39. P. M.

1. THE wondrous love of Jesus,
From doubts and fears it frees us,
With pitying love he sees us,
   A toiling here below:
Through tribulation driven,
We'll force our way to heaven;
Through consolation given,
   Rejoicing on we'll go.

2. Companions now distressed,
By Satan sore oppressed,
Cheer up, you'll be relieved,
   Your Captain's gone before:
In every trying hour,
He'll save you by his power,
And bring you safe to heaven,
   On that eternal shore.

3. O yonder is the glory,
It lies but just before you,
And there we'll tell the story
   Of all redeeming love:
And there we shall for ever,
Drink of that flowing river,
And ever, ever, ever,
   Surround the throne of love.

4. There in the blooming garden
   Of Eden, gain'd by pardon,
   Upon the banks of Jordan
     We will worship the Lamb:
   We'll sing the song of Moses,
   While Jesus he composes
   A song that never closes,
     Of pleasures to his name.

HYMN 40. P. M.

1. THE reason we love friendship
     We will deny to no man,
   How shall, how shall, how shall we,
     Who are thus form'd for happiness,
   E'er slight a loving Christian,
     Since Jesus, Jesus, hath died on the tree,
   For to deliver man,
     From violence and treason:
   That we might love each other,
     And seek our soul's salvation.
   'Twas love that mov'd the mighty God
     For to redeem the nations,
   That happy, happy, they might be.

2. On the feast day in ancient times
     Jesus stood thus crying,
   Who so thirsteth, let ev'ry man
     Come unto me and freely drink,
   And thus be sav'd from dying:
     For surely, surely, nothing else can

Quench the immortal thirst
　That in your heart is glowing:
Come then and drink the streams of grace,
　Which are so freely flowing,
Saying, drink, my love, my only dove,
　For you it is a flowing—
Then happy, happy, you shall be.

2. Let us, who have begun to taste
　The sweets of this salvation,
Follow, follow, let us follow on,
　Believing we shall overcome,
Resisting all temptation:
　Since Jesus, Jesus, since Jesus the Son,
With outstretched arms,
　And voice that's so inviting,
To purling streams of purest joys,
　Is thus our souls exciting,
Let us impart to him our hearts,
　By faith and love uniting,
Then happy, happy, we shall be,

HYMN 41.　P. M.

1. COME all ye weary travellers,
　　And let us join to sing,
　The everlasting praises
　　Of Jesus Christ, our king;
　We've had a tedious journey,
　　And tiresome, 'tis true;
　But see how many dangers
　　The Lord has brought us through

2. At first when Jesus found us,
   He call'd us unto him;
And pointed out the danger
   Of falling into sin:
The world, the flesh and Satan,
   Will prove a fatal snare,
Unless we do reject them,
   By faith and humble prayer.

3. But by our disobedience,
   With sorrow we confess,
We've had too long to wander
   In a dark wilderness;
Where we might soon have fainted,
   In that enchanted ground;
But now and then a cluster
   Of pleasant grapes we found.

4. The pleasant fruits of Canaan,
   Give life, and joy, and peace;
Revive our drooping spirits,
   And faith and love increase;
Confess our Lord and Master,
   And run at his command;
And hasten on our journey
   Unto the promis'd land.

5. In faith and hope, and patience,
   We now are going on,
The pleasant way to Canaan,
   Where Jesus Christ is gone;

In peace and consolation,
  We're going to rejoice;
And Jesus and his people
  For ever be our choice.

6. Sinners, why stand ye idle,
  While we do march along?
Has conscience never told you,
  That you are going wrong;
Down the broad road to ruin,
  To bear an endless curse?
Forsake your ways of sinning,
  And come along with us.

7. But if you will refuse us,
  We'll bid you all farewell;
We're on the way to Canaan,
  And you the way to hell;
We're sorry for to leave you,
  We'd rather you would go;
Come try a bleeding Saviour,
  And feel salvation flow.

8. O sinners, be awaken'd
  To see your dismal state;
Repent and be converted,
  Before it is too late;
Turn to the Lord by praying,
  And daily search his word;
And never rest contented,
  Until you find the Lord.

9. Now to the king immortal,
   Be everlasting praise,
For in his holy service
   We mean to spend our days;
   Till we arrive at Canaan,
     The celestial world above,
With everlasting praises,
   To sing redeeming love.

HYMM 42. P. M

Union with Christ.

1. COME, saints and sinners, hear me tell,
   The wonders of Immanuel;
   Who sav'd me from a burning hell,
   And brought my soul with him to dwell,
     And gave me heavenly union.

2. When Jesus saw me from on high,
   Beheld my soul in ruin lie,
   He look'd on me with pitying eye,
   And said to me as he pass'd by,
     With God you have no union.

3. Then I began to weep and pray,
   I look'd this way and that to fly,
   It griev'd me sore that I must die,
   I sought salvation for to buy,
     But still I found no union.

4. But when I hated all my sin
   My dear Redeemer took me in,

And with his blood he wash'd me clean,
And O! what seasons I have seen,
  Ever since I felt this union.

5. I prais'd the Lord both night and day,
I went from house to house to pray,
And if I met one on the way,
I always found something to say,
  About this heavenly union.

6. I wonder why old saints don't sing,
And praise the Lord upon the wing,
And make the heavenly arches ring,
With loud hosannas to our king,
  Who brought our souls to union.

7. Come, poor backslider, come away,
And mind to do as well as say,
And learn to watch as well as pray,
And bear your cross from day to day,
  And then you'll feel this union.

8. O, could I like an angel sound,
Salvation through the earth around,
The devil's kingdon to confound,
I'd triumph on Immanuel's ground,
  And spread this heavenly union.

9. Come, heaven and earth, unite your lays,
And give to Jesus endless praise,
And thou, my soul, look on and gaze,
He weeps, he bleeds, thy debt he pays,
  To give thee heavenly union.

10. We soon shall leave all things below,
And quit this vale of pain and woe,
And then we'll all to glory go,
And there we'll see, and hear, and know,
And feel a perfect union.

11. There we the glorious Lamb shall see,
Who groan'd and died upon the tree,
Who spill'd his blood to set us free,
That we might his salvation see,
And feel a gracious union.

12. Almighty God, teach heart and tongue,
To thee to raise a grateful song,
All praises to thy name belong,
Let Zion sing, thy kingdom come,
And fill the world with union.

HYMN 43. P. M.

1 FAR above yon glorious ceiling
Of the azure vaulted sky,
Jesus sits, his love revealing,
To his splendid troops on high.

2. Hosts seraphic humbly bowing,
At his feet they prostrate fall;
Saints and angels all avowing,
God in Christ is all in all.

3. Could we leave our foolish dreaming
   Of a fancied heaven below,
 And see Jesu's glory beaming,
   How our souls would long to go.

4. Earth by us would then be spurned,
     All its vanity subside;
 Fuel fit for to burned,
     All its honours, pleasures, pride.

5. From the general conflagration,
     We should to God's refuge fly;
 Clasp the hope of our salvation,
     Live in Christ, in Jesus die.

6. We in him our rest regaining,
     All its blessedness should prove;
 O'er our foes victorious reigning,
     Perfected in spotless love.

7. We should for his day be waiting,
     When the full reward is given;
 When the glorious work's completed,
     Jesus takes his church to heaven.

8. Pure from every stain of nature,
     There in holiness to shine;
 Moulded like its great Creator,
     All immortal, all divine.

HYMN 44. P. M.

The Jubilee.

1 HARK! the jubilee is sounding;
   O the joyful news is come:

Free salvation is proclaimed,
  In and through God's own dear Son;
Now we have an invitation
  To the meek and lowly Lamb;
Glory, honour, and salvation,
  Christ the Lord is come to reign.

2. Come dear friend and don't neglect it,
    Come to Jesus in your prime;
  Great salvation, don't reject it,
    O receive it, now's your time;
  Now the Saviour is beginning
    To revive his work again;
  Glory, honour, and Salvation,
    Christ the Lord is come to reign.

3. Come, dear children, praise your Jesus,
    Praise him, praise him evermore,
  May his great love now constrain us,
    His great name for to adore;
  O then let us join together,
    Crowns of glory to obtain;
  Glory, honor, and salvation,
    Christ the Lord is come to reign.

HYMN 45. P. M,

[By the late Rev. G. Askins.]

1. BRETHERN, we have met to worship
    And adore the Lord our God;
  Will you pray with all your power,
    While we try to preach the word?

All is vain unless the Spirit
  Of the Holy One comes down:
Brethren, pray, and holy manna
  Will be shower'd all around.

2. Brethren, see poor sinners round you
  Slumbering on the brink of woe;
Death is coming, hell is moving,
  Can you bear to let them go?
See our fathers, and our mothers,
  And our children sinking down:
Brethren, pray, and holy manna
  Will be shower'd all around.

3. Brethren, here are poor backsliders,
  Who were once near heaven's door,
But they have betray'd their Saviour,
  And are worse than e'er before;
Yet the Saviour offers pardon,
  If they will lament their wound;
Brethren, pray and holy manna
  Will be shower'd all around.

4. Sisters, will you join and help, like
  Moses' sisters helped him,
While you see the trembling sinners,
  Who are struggling hard with sin?
Tell them all about the Saviour,
  Tell them that he will be found:
Pray on, sisters, and the manna
  Will be shower'd all around.

5. Let us love our God supremely,
  Let us love each other too,

Let us love and pray for sinners,
 'Till our God makes all things new;
Then he'll call us home to heaven,
 At his table we'll sit down:
Christ will gird himself and serve us
 With sweet manna all around.

HYMN 47. P. M.

1. O JESUS, now thy power display,
 And stir us up to watch and pray;
That we at last may hear thee say,
Come, reign with me in endless day,
 And feel eternal union.

2, Come, brethren, let us heavenward go,
 Until we end our race below,
Then we shall leave this world of wo,
 And everlasting pleasures know,
 And feel immortal union.

3. Our race is short, 'twill soon be o'er,
Then we shall weep and sigh no more,
And join the saints on Canaan's shore,
The name of Jesus to adore,
 And feel that endless union.

Then when this mortal frame shall die,
And long in death's embraces lie,
My soul to realms of bliss shall fly,
And sing and shout beyond the sky,
 And feel that heav'nly union.

5. And when to that bright world I come,
And gain my everlasting home,
My soul shall there for ever bloom,
Until my body leaves the tomb,
    Then both shall join that union.

HYMN 48   P M.

1. O JESUS, my Saviour, I know thou art mine,
    For thee all the pleasures of earth I resign
Thou art my rich treasure, my joy and my love,
    Nothing richer possess'd by the angels above.

2. Thy spirit first taught me to know I was blind,
    Then taught me the way of salvation to find;
And when I was sinking in gloomy despair,
    My Jesus relieved me and bid me not fear.

3. In vain I attempt to describe what I feel,
    The language of mortals here ever must fail :
My Jesus is precious, my soul's in a flame,
    I am raised into raptures while praising his name.

4. I find him in singing, he is present in prayer,
    In sweet meditation he always is near;
My constant companion, may we never part;
    All glory to Jesus, he dwells in my heart.

5. If ever I lov'd thee, 'tis now my dear Lord,
   I love thy dear children, thy ways and thy word;
  I love all creation, I love sinners too,
   Since Jesus has died to redeem them from wo.

6. When happy in Jesus, I cannot forbear,
   Though sinners despise me, his love to declare;
  His love overwhelms me, had I wings I would fly,
   And praise him in mansions prepared on high.

HYMN 49. P. M.

1. WHAT happy children, who follow Jesus
   Into the house of prayer and praise;
  And join in union, while love increases,
   Resolved this way to spend our days:
  Altho' we're hated by the world and Satan,
   By the flesh, and such as love not God;
  Yet happy moments and joyful seasons,
   We oft times find on Canaan's road.

2. Since we've been waiting on lovely Jesus
   We've felt some strength come from above;
  Our hearts have burned with holy rapture,
   We long to be absorbed by love:
  Then let us hold fast what is given,
   And trust in God for time to come:

Sure we shall find our way to heaven,
So farewell, brethren, we're going home.

3. And as we go, let us praise our Jesus,
And pray for those who spurn his grace;
Lest they should lose love's richest treasure,
And ne'er enjoy his smiling face;
Now here's my heart and my best wishes,
In token of my Christian love;
In hopes with you to praise my Jesus,
So farewell, brethren, we'll meet above.

HYMN 50. P. M.

1. AWAKE! O guilty world, awake!
Behold the earth's foundation shake!
While the Redeemer bleeds for you:
His death proclaims to all our race,
Free grace, free grace, free grace, free grace
To all the Jews and Gentiles too!

2. Come, guilty mortals, come and see;
Your Saviour hanging on the tree!
For you all drest in purple gore,
His weight of woe did veil the sun!
'Tis done, 'tis done, 'tis done, 'tis done,
That man might live for evermore!

3. Behold the wounded Lamb of God!
Spreading his bleeding hands abroad!
Come see him yielding up to death!

Behold him in his agonies!
He dies! he dies! he dies! he dies!
   And yields his last expiring breath!

4. He dies and triumphs over death,
To give the dead immortal breath,
   And spread the wonders of his name!
Shout, brethren, shout with cheerful voice,
Rejoice, rejoice, rejoice, rejoice,
   And give the glory to the Lamb.

HYMN 51. C. M.

1. OUR souls by love together knit,
   Cemented mix'd in one;
One hope, one heart, one mind, one voice,
   'Tis heav'n on earth begun:
Our hearts have burnt while Jesus spoke,
   And glow'd with sacred fire:
He stopp'd and talk'd, and fed and blest,
   And fill'd the enlarged desire.

CHORUS.

A Saviour, let creation sing;
A Saviour, let all heaven ring;
He's God with us, we feel him ours;
His fulness in our souls he pours;
'Tis almost done, 'tis almost o'er;
We're joining those who're gone before;
We then shall meet to part no more.

We're soldiers fighting for our God,
   Let trembling cowards fly;
We'll stand unshaken, firm and fix'd,
   With Christ to live and die:
Let devils rage and men assail,
   We'll cut our passage through:
Let foes unite, and friends desert,
   We'll seize the crown, our due.
              A Saviour, &c.

The little cloud increases still!
   The heav'ns are big with rain;
We haste to catch the teeming shower,
   And all its moisture drain:
A rill, a stream, a torrent flows,
   But pour the mighty flood;
O sweep the nations, shake the earth,
   'Till all proclaim thee God.
              A Saviour, &c.

And when thou mak'st thy jewels up,
   And set'st thy starry crown;
When all thy sparkling gems shall shine,
   Proclaim'd by thee thine own;
May we, a little band of love,
   We sinners sav'd by grace,
From glory, into glory chang'd,
   Behold thee face to face.
              A Saviour, &c.

HYMN 52. P. M.

1. IN the house of king David a fountain did spring,
   For sin and uncleanness, from Jesus our king;
   This fountain flows sweetly, whenever applied,
   It sprang from the bowels of Christ, when he died.

2. Come all that have bath'd in the fountain of love,
   And have felt th' heavy burthen of guilt to remove;
   Let's praise our dear Saviour, as long as we've breath,
   And after we're laid in the dust of the earth.

3. There, there, we shall sleep, but not always remain,
   We look for the coming of Jesus again;
   When wak'd by the trumpet, we'll lay by our shrouds,
   And rise to meet Jesus, our Lord, in the clouds.

4. How we shall be fashion'd, he does not declare,
   But we shall be like him, when he doth appear;
   And that happy moment we're longing to see,
   When we shall be perfectly happy in thee.

5. Lord Jesus I love thee thou knowest very well,
   Assist me to conquer the powers of hell;
   Though Satan he rages, and frightens me too,
   Lord Jesus protect me, and bring me safe through.

HYMN 53. C. M.

1. ARISE and shine, O Zion fair,
     Behold thy light is come;
   Thy glorious conq'ring king is near,
     To take his exiles home:
   The trumpet sounding through the sky,
     To set poor captives free;
   The day of wonder now is nigh,
     The year of jubilee.

2. Ye heralds blow your trumpets loud,
     The earth must know her doom;
   Go spread the news from pole to pole,
     Behold the judge is come:
   Blow out the sun! burn up the earth!
     Consume the rolling flood!
   While every star shall disappear;
     Go turn the moon to blood!

3. Arise ye nations under ground,
     Before the judge appear;
   All tongues and languages shall come,
     Their final doom to hear!

King Jesus on his dazzling throne,
  Ten thousand angels round;
And Gabriel with a silver trump,
  Echo's the awful sound!

4 The glorious news of gospel grace
  To sinners now is o'er;
The trump in Zion now is still,
  And to be heard no more!
The watchmen all have left their walls,
  And with their flocks above,
On Canaan's peaceful shore they sing,
  And shout redeeming love!

SECOND PART. C. M.

1. COME on, my brethren in the Lord,
    Whose hearts are joined in one;
  Hold up your heads with courage bold,
    Your race is almost run:
  Above the clouds, behold him stand,
    And smiling bids you come;
  And angels whisp'ring you away,
    To your eternal home.

2. To see a pilgrim as he dies,
    With glory in his view;
  To heav'n, he lifts his longing eyes,
    And bids the world adieu,
  While friends are weeping all around,
    And loth to let him go;
  He shouts with his expiring breath,
    And leaves them all below!

3. O Christians are you ready now,
   To cross the swelling flood;
On Canaan's happy shore to stand,
   And see your smiling God!
The dazzling charms of that bright world,
   Attracts my soul above!
My tongue shall shout redeeming grace,
   When perfected in love.

4. Go on, my brethren in the Lord,
   I'm bound to meet you there;
Although we tread enchanted ground,
   Be bold and never fear:
Fight on, fight on, ye valiant souls,
   The land appears in view;
I hope to gain fair Canaan's shore,
   And there to meet with you.

HYMN 54. C. M.

1. SWEET rivers of redeeming love,
   Lie just before mine eye;
Had I the pinions of a dove.
   I'd to those rivers fly:
I'd rise superior to my pain,
   With joy out strip the wind;
I'd cross bold Jordan's stormy main,
   And leave the world behind.

2. While I'm imprison'd here below,
   In anguish, pain, and smart,
Oft times those troubles I forego,
   When love surrounds my heart:

In darkest shadows of the night,
  Faith mounts the upper sky,
I then behold my heart's delight,
  And would rejoice to die!

3. I view the monster death, and smile,
  Now he has lost his sting;
Though Satan rages all the while
  I still in triumph sing:
I hold my Saviour in my arms,
  And will not let him go;
I'm so delighted with his charms,
  No other good I'll know.

4. A few more years, or days at most,
  My troubles will be o'er,
I hope to join the heav'nly host,
  On Canaan's happy shore.
My rapt'rous soul shall drink and feast,
  In love's unbounded sea;
The glorious hope of endless rest,
  Is transporting to me.

5. O come, my Saviour, come away,
  And bear me through the sky,
Nor let thy chariot wheels delay,
  Make haste, and bring it nigh:
I long to see thy glorious face,
  And in thine image shine;
To triumph in victorious grace,
  And be for ever thine.

6. Then I will tune my harp of gold,
   To my eternal king;
Through ages that can ne'er be told,
   I'll make his praises ring:
All hail! thou great eternal God!
   Who died on Calvary;
And sav'd me with thy precious blood,
   From endless misery.

7. Ten thousand, thousand join in one,
   To praise the Eternal Three:
Prostrate before the blazing throne,
   In deep humility:
They rise and tune their harp of gold,
   And string the immortal lyre;
And ages that can ne'er be told,
   Shall raise their praises higher.

HYMN 55. P. M.

1. ARISE and hail the sacred day,
Cast all low cares of life away,
   And thoughts of meaner things:
This day to cure our deadly woes
The son of righteousness arose
   With healing in his wings.

2. If angels, on that happy morn
The Saviour of the world was born,
   Pour'd forth seraphic songs:
Much more should we, of human race,
Adore the wonders of his grace,
   To whom the grace belongs.

3. How wonderful, how vast his love,
   Who left the shining realms above;
      Those happy seats of rest:
   How much for lost mankind he bore,
   Their peace and pardon to restore,
      Can never be express'd.

4. While we adore his boundless grace,
   And pious joy and mirth takes place
      Of sorrow, grief and pain,
   Give glory to our God on high,
   And not amidst the gen'ral joy,
      Forget good will to men.

5. O then, let heaven and earth rejoice,
   Creation's whole united voice,
      And hymn that happy day,
   When sin and Satan vanquish'd fell,
   And all the pow'rs of death and hell
      Before his sov'reign sway.

HYMN. 56. C. M.

The Saviour's call.

1 SINNER, hear the Saviour's call,
      He now is passing by;
   He has seen thy grievous thrall,
      And heard thy mournful cry;
   He has pardons to impart,
      Grace to save thee from thy fears,
   See the love that fills his heart,
      And wipes away thy tears.

2. Why art thou afraid to come,
   And tell him all thy case?
He will not pronounce thy doom,
   Nor frown thee from his face:
Wilt thou fear Immanuel?
   Wilt thou fear the Lamb of God,
Who to save thy soul from hell
   Has shed his precious blood?

3. Think, how on the cross he hung,
   Pierced with a thousand wounds!
Hark from each as with a tongue,
   The voice of pardon sounds!
See from all his bursting veins,
   Blood of wond'rous virtue flow!
Shed to wash away thy stain,
   And ransom thee from woe.

4. Though his majesty be great,
   His mercy is no less;
Though he thy transgressions hate,
   He feels for thy distress:
By himself the Lord has sworn,
   He delights not in thy death,
But invites thee to return,
   That thou may'st live by faith

5 Raise thy down-cast eyes and see,
   What throngs his throne surround,
These, though sinners once like thee,
   Have full salvation found;
Yield not then to unbelief!
   While he says, "There yet is room;"
Though of sinners thou art chief,
   Since Jesus calls thee home.

HYMN 57. P. M.

1 THE sacred ties of friendship
Unite all loving Christians,
In glory, in glory, they shall live;
No time nor place shall change them,
And death shall ne'er dissolve them,
United, united, are they that believe:
When Gabriel's trumpet sounding,
And conquered death resigning,
The scattered dust uniting,
The soul and body joining;
All join the grand procession,
And glory realizing,
Then happy, happy, we shall be.

2 The bliss exquisite flowing,
The friends of Jesus shouting,
Such raptures, raptures flow from his word;
The angels join in concert,
While Jesus stands inviting,
Come on, come on, ye blessed of the Lord,
Behold the crowns of glory:
And saints and angels meeting,
And living streams of purest joys,
For ever are increasing:
In azure fields for ever range,
And view a smiling Jesus,
Then happy, happy, we shall be.

3 The sinner's now lamenting,
He sees the grand procession,

A marching, marching, to the dazzling throne:
His frightful soul alarm'd,
He cries with looks amaz'd,
Farewell, farewell, I'm for ever gone:
Behold a godly father,
And there's a pious mother,
How did they pray together,
They float on streams of pleasure,
And I am lost for ever;
On waves of endless sorrow,
Then torments, torments, are for ever mine.

HYMN 58. C. M.

1 ATTEND, young friends, while I relate
    The dangers you are in,
The evils that around you wait,
    While subject unto sin.
Although you flourish like the rose,
    While in its branches green,
Your sparkling eyes in death must close,
    No more for to be seen.

2 In silent shades you must lie down,
    Long in your graves to dwell,
Your friends will then stand weeping round,
    And bid a long farewell.
How small this world will then appear
    At that tremendous hour,
When you Jehovah's voice shall hear,
    And feel his mighty power.

3. In vain you'll mourn your days are past,
    Alas those days are gone,
  Your golden hours are spent at last,
    And never to return.
  O come this moment and begin,
    While life's sweet moments last,
  Turn to the Lord, forsake all sin,
    And he'll forgive what's past.

HYMN 59. P. M.

The Balm of Gilead.

1. THERE shall we reign with Jesus, on that delightful shore,
    And shout with the redeemed, our trials are all o'er;
    The wicked cease from troubling, the weary are at rest,
    And we shall reign with Jesus, eternal ages blest.

2. We shall be like the angels, in that immortal throng,
    And shout aloud salvation, 'twill be our lasting song;
    They sing creating goodness, and we redeeming love,
    And this shall be our business, in the bright worlds above.

3. This love so freely flowing, it animates our hearts,
   This love is still abounding, in every place and part;
   This love can ne'er be ended, though faith and hope should cease,
   This love can ne'er be bounded, but ever will increase.

4. This love through endless ages, it ever is the same,
   'Tis this our heart engages, to love and serve the Lamb:
   Unites us altogether, and makes us of one soul,
   It is the Balm of Gilead, it makes the wounded whole.

HYMN 60. C. M.

The Zion Traveller

1. YE weary, heavy laden souls,
   Who are oppressed sore,
  Ye trav'llers through the wilderness,
   To Canaan's peaceful shore:
  Through chilling winds, and beating rain,
   The waters deep and cold,
  And enemies surrounding you,
   Take courage and be bold.

2. Though storms and hurricanes arise,
   The desert all around,
And fiery serpents oft appear
   Through the enchanted ground :
Dark nights and clouds and gloomy fear,
   And dragons often roar;
But while the gospel trump we hear
   We'll press for Canaan's shore.

3. We're often like the lonesome dove,
   Who mourns her absent mate;
From hill to hill, from vale to vale,
   Her sorrows to relate ;
But Canaan's land is just before,
   Sweet spring is coming on,
A few more beating winds and rains,
   And winter will be gone.

4. Sometimes like mountains to the sky,
   Black Jordan's billows roar,
Which often makes the pilgrims fear,
   They never will get o'er :
But let us gain mount Pisgah's top,
   And view the vernal plain,
To fright our souls, may Jordan roar,
   And hell may rage in vain.

5. Methinks I now begin to see
   The borders of that land;
The trees of life, with heav'nly fruit,
   In beauteous order stand:
The wint'ry time is past and gone,
   Sweet flowers doth appear,
The fiftieth year hath now rolled round,
   The great Sabbatick year.

6. O, what a glorious sight appears,
   To my believing eyes;
Methinks I see Jerusalem,
   A city in the skies:
Bright angels whisp'ring me away,
   "O come, my brother, come,"
And I am willing to be gone
   To my eternal home.

7. Farewell, my brethren in the Lord,
   Who are to Canaan bound:
And should we never meet again
   'Till the jubilee trump shall sound,
I hope that I shall meet you there,
   On that delightful shore;
In oceans of eternal bliss,
   Where parting is no more.

HYMN 61. P. M.

1. HARK! my soul, it is the Lord,
'Tis thy Saviour, hear his word;
Jesus speaks, and speaks to thee,
Say, poor sinner, "Lov'st thou me?"

2. "I delivered thee, when bound,
And when wounded, heal'd thy wound,
Sought thee wandering, set thee right,
Turn'd thy darkness into light.

3. "Can a woman's tender care
Cease towards the child she bear:

Yes! she may forgetful be,
Yet I will remember thee.

4. "Mine is an unchanging love,
Higher than the heights above,
Deeper than the depths beneath,
Free and faithful, strong as death.

5 "Thou shalt see my glory soon,
When the work of grace is done,
Partner of my throne shall be,
Say, poor sinner, lov'st thou me?"

6 Lord, it is my chief complaint,
That my love is weak and faint;
Yet I love thee, and adore,
O for grace to love thee more.

HYMN 62. P. M.

1 FAREWELL, my dear brethren, the time is at hand,
That we must part from this social band;
Our several engagements now call us away,
Our parting is needful, and we must obey.

2 Farewell, my dear brethren, farewell for a while,
We'll soon meet again, if kind providence smile;

But when we are parted, and scattered abroad,
We'll pray for each other when wrestling with God.

3 Farewell, faithful soldiers, you'll soon be discharg'd,
The war will be ended, your treasures enlarged;
With shouting and singing, tho' Jordan may roar.
We'll enter fair Canaan, and rest on the shore.

4 Farewell, ye young converts, who're listed for war,
Sore trials await you, but Jesus is near;
Altho' you must travel the dark wilderness,
Your captain's before you, he'll lead you to peace.

5 The world and the devil, and hell all unite,
And bold persecution will try you to fright;
But Jesus stands for you, who is stronger than they,
Let this animate you to march on your way.

6 Farewell, seeking mourners, with sad broken hearts,
O hasten to Jesus, and choose the good part,
He's full of compassion, and mighty to save,
His arms are extended your souls to receive.

7 Farewell, faithful Christians, farewell all around,
Perhaps we'll not meet till the last trump shall sound;
To meet you in glory, I'll give you my hand,
Our Saviour to praise in a pure social band.

HYMN 63. P. M.

1 FAREWELL, my dear brethren, I bid you farewell,
I'm going to travel the way to excel;
I'm going to travel the wilderness through,
Therefore, my dear brethren, I bid you adieu.

2 The thoughts of our parting doth cause me to grieve,
So well do I love you, but you I must leave;
My Jesus commands, and I must obey,
Therefore, my dear brethren, don't grieve after me.

3 May the heavens protect you, be Jesus your guide,
On the walls of our Zion may you ever abide;
Though we live at a distance, and you I ne'er see,
On the banks of sweet Canaan acquainted we'll be.

4 There all things are plenty, and the leaves growing green,
And the parting of Christians no more to be seen;

No sorrow, no trouble, shall enter that place,
But there we shall join in a song of free grace.

5 And when we meet Jesus in the mansions above,
Where saints and bright angels are feasting on love;
O then we shall look for each mourner that's here,
How glad we shall be to meet each other there.

6 Farewell to all sorrows, temptations and pain,
I'm going where Jesus for ever doth reign;
I'm going to Jesus, his goodness to prove,
Where saints and bright angels are feasting on love.

HYMN 64. L. M.

1 COME, my soul, thy suit prepare,
Jesus loves to answer prayer;
He himself has bid thee pray,
Therefore will not say thee nay.

2 Thou art coming to a king,
Large petitions with thee bring:
For his grace and power are such,
None can ever ask too much.

3 With my burden I begin,
Lord, remove this load of sin!
Let thy blood for sinners spilt,
Set my conscience free from guilt.

4 Lord, I come to thee for rest,
Take possession of my breast;
There thy blood-bought right maintain,
And without a rival reign.

5 As the image in the glass,
Answers the beholder's face,
Thus unto my heart appear,
Print thine own resemblance there.

6 While I am a pilgrim here,
Let thy love my spirit cheer;
As my guide, my guard, my friend,
Lead me to my journey's end.

7 Shew me what I have to do,
Every hour my strength renew;
Let me live a life of faith,
Let me die thy people's death.

HYMN 65. C. M.

1 HOW sweet, how heavenly is the sight,
When those that love the Lord,
In one another's peace delight,
And so fulfil his word.

2 When each can feel his brother's sigh,
And with him bear a part;
When sorrows flow from eye to eye,
And joy from heart to heart.

3 When, free from envy, scorn and pride,
Our wishes all above,
Each can his brother's failings hide,
And show a brother's love.

4 When love, in one delightful stream,
Through every bosom flows;
When union sweet, and dear esteem,
In every action glows.

5 Love is the golden chain that binds
The happy souls above;
And he's an heir of heaven that finds
His bosom glow with love.

HYMN 66. P. M.

1 LORD, my ransom'd soul adores thee;
Thou my joy and portion art:
Day and night I plead before thee—
Answer Lord—thy grace impart.
    Send thy Spirit,
Pierce the stubborn sinner's heart.

2 Ah! dear Lord, they're bound for ruin,
Hast'ning down to endless woe:
While their danger we are viewing,
Streams of briny sorrow flow.
    Lord, alarm them,
Or to ruin they must go!

3 See, dear Lord, our near connexions,
　Dear companions all around,
Brothers, sisters, children, parents,
　Down to desperation bound.
　　　　　Jesus, save them;
　Let the lost again be found.

4 Prayers and tears, alas! we've vented;
　Shall we weep and pray in vain?
Yet alas! they seem contented!
　Nought but scoffs and frowns we gain.
　　　　　Jesus, save them;
　Save them, Lord, from endless pain.

5 Death, it may be now, is near them;
　Soon they'll feel his cold embrace:
Gracious heaven! shall we hear them
　Mourn thy long rejected grace?
　　　　　Lord, constrain them
　Now to seek a Saviour's face.

6 Lord, we view the separation
　At thy great, tremendous bar:
Mourning, weeping, lamentation,
　Must be their employment there.
　　　　　Must we see them
　Stand their awful doom to hear?

7 Must we there be separated,
　Never, never more to meet?
Mournful scene, long contemplated!
　Lord and is there mercy yet?
　　　　　Lay them prostrate,
　Precious Jesus, at thy feet.

8 Lord display thy matchless power,
 Pierce their stubborn hearts of stone,
Make them dread that awful hour—
 Bow them, Lord, before thy throne.
   Save them, Jesus;
 Save them, save them for thine own.

HYMN 67. P M.

The happy Pilgrim,

1 I LOVE my blessed Saviour,
 I feel I'm in his favour,
 And I am his for ever
  If I but faithful prove;
 And now I'm bound for Canaan
 I feel my sins forgiv'n,
 And soon shall get to heaven
  To sing redeeming love.

2 Poor sinners may deride me,
 And unbelievers chide me,
 But nothing shall divide me,
  From Jesus my friend.
 Supported by his power,
 I long to see the hour,
 That bids my spirit tower,
  And all my troubles end.

3 The pleasing time is hast'ning,
 My tott'ring frame is wasting,
 While I'm engaged in praising,
  Impelled by his love.

When yonder shining orders,
Who sing on Canaan's borders,
Shall bear me to their Lord, there
  To praise him above.

4 My thirsty soul is panting,
My body almost fainting,
While praise and prayer are venting,
  From my feeble tongue.
How ardent my desire,
Lord Jesus, raise me higher,
To join the holy choir,
  In that immortal song.

5 Farewell, I'm bound for glory,
How pleasing is the story!
Those shining worlds before me
  Invite me to be gone.
Had I angels' pinions
I'd range the bright dominions,
And join the shining millions,
  Who're shouting round the throne

6 The pleasing smile of Jesus,
The rapturous sound increases,
And tunes the heav'nly voices
  Throughout the ethereal plains,
My flesh and spirit failing,
My soul in transports hailing,
Bright seraphs in their dwelling,
  I sing immortal strains.

HYMN 68. P. M.

1 MY days, my weeks, my months, my years,
Fly rapid as the whirling spheres,
  Around the steady pole;
Time, like the tide, its motion keeps,
And I must launch through endless deeps,
  Where endless ages roll.

2 The grave is near the cradle seen,
How swift the moments pass between,
  And whisper as they fly,
"Unthinking man, remember this,
Though fond of sublunary bliss,
  That you must groan and die."

3 My soul attend the solemn call,
Thine earthly tent must shortly fall,
  And thou must take thy flight;
Beyond the vast expansive blue,
To sing above as angels do,
  Or sink in endless night.

4 How great the bliss, how great the woe,
Hangs on this inch of time below,
  On this precarious breath;
The Lord of nature only knows,
Whether another year shall close,
  Ere I expire in death.

5 Long ere the sun shall run his round,
I may be buried under ground,
  And there in silence rot;

Alas! an hour may close the scene,
And ere twelve months shall roll between,
  My name be quite forgot.

6 But will my soul be thus extinct,
And cease to live, and cease to think?
  It cannot, cannot be;
No, my immortal connot die,
What wilt thou do, or whither fly,
  When death shall set thee free.

7 Will mercy then her arms extend,
Will Jesus be thy guardian friend,
  And heav'n thy dwelling place;
Or shall insulting fiends appear,
And drag thee down to dark despai
  Below the reach of grace?

8 A heav'n or hell, and these alone,
Beyond the present life are known,
  There is no middle space;
To-day attend the call divine,
To-morrow may be none of thine,
  Or it may be too late.

9 O do not pass this as a dream,
Vast is the change, whate'er it seem,
  To poor unthinking man:
Lord at thy footstool I would bow,
Bid conscience plainly tell me now,
  What it would tell me then.

10 If in destruction's road I stray;
  Help me to chose the better way,
    That leads to joys on nigh;
  Thy grace impart, my guilt forgive,
  Nor let me ever dare to live,
    Such as I dare not die.

HYMN 69. P. M.

1 I LOVE thee, I love thee, I love thee, my love,
  I long thy salvation more fully to prove;
  I love thee, I love thee, I love thee, O why?
  Because my dear Saviour for sinners did die.

2 On Zion's bright mountain this news I will tell,
  The strains of redemption my bosom shall swell,
  With angelic ardour his love I'll proclaim,
  Redemption for sinners in Jesus's name.

3 Redemption, redemption, thro' Zion shall ring,
  In the flame of redemption, her converts shall sing;
  Redemption, redemption, through Jesus's blood,
  Descending from Calv'ry, and runs like a flood.

4 We'll talk of redemption while we stay below,
  We'll sing of redemption when upwards we go;

When the sun shall be darken'd, the moon turn'd to blood,
We'll shout full redemption in the kingdom of God.

5 When sinking in sorrow free grace did abound,
Pursu'd by the devil, redemption we found;
Our hearts to redemption we'll tune ev'ry string,
Thro' heaven's high arches redemption shall ring.

6 Redemption, redemption, to him that was slain,
We'll out sing the angels in this heavenly strain,
Redemption to Jesus, for ever we'll cry,
For men, not for angels, the Saviour did die.

7 All glory, all glory, to Jesus's name,
All wisdom and power to the spotless Lamb;
To him that redeem'd us, the great One in Three,
Hosannah, hosannah, through eternity.

8 The song of creation bright angels may sing,
But we'll sing redemption to Christ our king,
Thro' eternal ages these songs shall be sung,
While Jesus's glory inspires each tongue.

HYMN 70. C. M.

1 WITH love and pity I look round,
   Upon my fellow clay,
 See men reject the gospel sound,
   In this enlightened day!
 O sinner, sinner, will you hear,
   When in God's name I come?
 Upon your peril don't forbear,
   Lest hell should be your doom.

2 Now is the time, the accepted hour,
   O sinner, come away,
 The Saviour's knocking at your door,
   Arise without delay:
 O don't refuse to give him room,
   Lest mercy should withdraw;
 He'll then in robes of vengeance come
   To execute his law.

3 Then where poor sinner, will you be,
   If destitute of grace,
 When you your injured Judge shall see,
   And stand before his face?
 O! could you shun that dreadful sight,
   How would you wish to fly
 To the dark shades of endless night,
   From his all-searching eye.

4 But death and hell must all appear,
   And you among them stand,
 Before that great impartial bar,
   Arranged at Christ's left hand;

No yearning bowels pity then,
  Will ere affect my heart—
No—I shall surely say amen,
  When Christ bids you depart,

5 Let not these warnings be in vain,
  But lend a listening ear,
Lest you should meet them all again,
  When wrapt in keen despair.
Come lovely youth, embrace the truth,
  And join with one accord,
And use your tongue, while you are young,
  In praising of the Lord.

HYMN 71. C. M.

1. AFFLICTIONS, though they seem severe,
    In mercy oft are sent,
  They stopp'd the prodigal's career,
    And caused him to repent.

2. Although he no relentings felt,
    'Till he had spent his store,
  His stubborn heart began to melt,
    When famine pinch'd him sore.

3. "What have I gain'd by sin," he said,
    "But hunger, shame, and fear?
  My father's house abounds with bread,
    While I am starving here.

4. "I'll go and tell him all I've done,
    Fall down before his face,
  Unworthy to be call'd his son,
    I'll seek a servant's place."

5. His farther saw him coming back,
　　He saw, and ran, and smil'd;
　Then threw his arms around the neck
　　Of his rebellious child.

6. "Father, I've sinn'd, but O! forgive"—
　　"Enough," the father said,
　"Rejoice, my house, my son's alive,
　　For whom I mourn'd as dead.

7. "Now let the fatted calf be slain,
　　Go spread the news around,
　My son was dead, but lives again
　　Was lost, but now is found."

8. 'Tis thus the Lord his love reveals,
　　To call poor sinners home;
　More than a father's love he feels,
　　And welcomes all that come.

HYMN 72　P. M.

The Pilgrim.

1. RISE, my soul, and stretch thy wings,
　　Thy better portion trace,
　Rise from transitory things,
　　Towards heaven thy native place.
　Sun, and moon, and stars, decay,
　　Time will soon the earth remove;
　Rise, my soul, and haste away
　　To seats prepar'd above.

2. Rivers to the ocean run,
   Nor stay in all their course;
  Fires ascend and seek the sun,
   Both speed them to their source.
  So a soul that's born of God,
   Pants to see his glorious face:
  Upwards tends to his abode,
   To rest in his embrace.

3. Fly my riches, fly my cares,
   While I that course explore;
  Flatt'ring world with all your snares,
   Solicit me no more.
  Pilgrims fix not here their home,
   Strangers tarry but a night:
  When the last dear morn shall come,
   We'll rise to glorious light.

4. Cease, ye pilgrims, cease to mourn,
   Press onward to the prize,
  Soon the Saviour will return,
   Triumphant through the skies.
  Yet a season, and you'll know,
   Happy entrance will be given,
  All your sorrows left below,
   And earth exchang'd for heaven.

HYMN 73. L. M.

Union Hymn.

1. FROM whence does the union arise,
   That hatred is conquer'd by love?

It fastens our souls with such ties,
 That distance nor time can remove.

2. It cannot in Eden be found,
 Nor yet in a Paradise lost;
It grows on Immanuel's ground,
 And Jesu's dear blood it did cost

3. My friends once so dear unto me
 Our souls so united in love;
Where Jesus is gone we shall be,
 In yonder blest mansions above.

4. O! why then so loth for to part?
 Since there we shall soon meet again,
Engrav'd on Immanuel's heart,
 At a distance we cannot remain.

5. And then we shall see that bright day,
 And join with the angels above,
Set free from the prisons of clay,
 United in Jesus' love.

6. With Jesus we ever shall reign,
 And all his bright glory shall see,
Singing hallelujahs, amen;
 Amen! even so let it be.

HYMN 74   P. M.

1. THERE is a holy city,
 A happy world above,
Beyond the starry regions,
 Built by the God of love:

An everlasting temple,
   And saints array'd in white,
They serve their great Redeemer,
   They dwell with him in light.

2. This is no world of trouble,
   The God of peace is there,
He wipes away their sorrows,
   He banishes their care;
Their joys are still increasing,
   Their songs are ever new,
They praise the eternal Father,
   The Son and Spirit too.

3 The meanest child of glory
   Outshines the radiant sun;
But who can speak the splendour
   Of that eternal throne,
Where Jesus sits exalted,
   In godlike majesty?
The elders fall before him,
   The angels bend the knee.

4 Is this the man of sorrows,
   Who stood at Pilate's bar,
Condemn'd by haughty Herod,
   And by his men of war?
He seems a mighty conqueror,
   Who spoil'd the powers below,
And ransom'd many captives
   From everlasting woe.

5 The hosts of saints around him,
　　Proclaim his work of grace;
　The patriarchs and prophets,
　　And all the godly race;
　Who speak of fiery trials
　　And tortures on their way
　They came from tribulation,
　　To everlasting day.

6 Now with a holy transport,
　　They tell their suff'rings o'er,
　Their tears and their temptations,
　　And all the pains they bore;
　They turn and bow to Jesus,
　　Who gain'd their liberty:
　Amid our fiercest dangers,
　　Our lives are hid in thee.

7 Long time I was invited
　　To gain that heav'nly rest;
　Grace made no hard condition,
　　'Twas only to be bless'd;
　But earth's bewitching pleasures
　　Inclined me long to stay;
　I sought her dreams and shadows,
　　And joys that pass away.

8 But now it is my purpose
　　The better way to find;
　To serve my great Creator,
　　And leave my sins behind;

In guilt's seducing mazes
  I will no longer roam;
I' l give my soul to Jesus,
  Who brings the ransom'd home.

9 And what shall be my journey,
  How long I'll stay below,
Or what shall be my trials,
  Are not for me to know:
In every day of trouble,
  I'll raise my thoughts on high;
I'll think of the bright temple,
  And crowns above the sky.

HYMN 75. L. M.

1 YE saints of Jesus courage take,
Having enlisted, ne'er look back;
We're sure to find the Lord at hand,
While marching to the promis'd land.

CHORUS.

This is the way to heaven, hallelujah, &c.

2 Behold with joy from whence we came
We've passed thro' storms and fiery flames;
In vain hath Satan made his stand
To keep us from the promis'd land.
    This is the way to heaven, &c.

3 We're trav'lling through the wilderness,
And bound for everlasting bliss;
By faith in God we firm can stand,
And march away to the promis'd land.
This is the way to heaven, &c.

4 Our enemies of every kind,
O may we daily leave behind:
Protected by our Saviour's hand,
We're sure to reach the promis'd land.
This is the way to heaven, &c.

5 While on our journey here below,
We look beyond this vale of woe,
And pray and wait till Christ shall send,
To take us to the promis'd land.
This is the way to heaven, &c

6 Tho' storms may rise, and thunders roll,
Convulse the globe from pole to pole,
Undaunted still our souls shall stand,
For soon we'll reach the promis'd land.
This is the way to heaven, &c.

7 Quickly we'll cross the rolling flood
Divided by the rod of God;
Then shall our Joshua demand,
Possession of the promis'd land.
Then we shall reign in heaven, &c.

8 Our fellow pilgrims there shall meet,
And brethren shall each other greet,

Admiring angels round us stand,
And welcome home to the promis'd land.
> *Then we shall shout in heaven, &c.*

9 All tears shall then be wip'd away,
For there's no sorrow night nor day;
But all unite to adore the hand,
That brought us safe to the promis'd land.
> *Then we shall reign for ever, &c.*

10 The wearied trav'ller then shall rest,
His spirit with the ever-blest;
And ever praise the God who plan'd
The way to obtain the promis'd land.
> *There we shall reign for ever, &c.*

HYMN 76. C. M.

On the death of a Believer.

1 IN vain my fancy strives to paint
　The moment after death,
The glories that surround the saints,
　When yielding up their breath.

2 One gentle sigh their fetters breaks;
　We scarce can say, "They're gone!"
Before the willing spirit takes
　Her mansion near the throne.

3 Faith strives, but all its efforts fail,
　To trace her in her flight;
No eye can pierce within the veil
　Which hides the world of light.

4 Thus much, and this is all we know,
  They are completely blest.
Have done with sin, and care, and woe,
  And with their Saviour rest.

5 On harps of gold they praise his name,
  His face they always view:
Then let us follow'rs be of them,
  That we may praise him too.

6 Their faith and patience, love and zeal,
  Should make their mem'ry dear;
And Lord, do thou the prayers fulfil,
  They offered for us here.

7 While they have gain'd, we losers are,
  We miss them day by day;
But thou can'st every breach repair,
  And wipe our tears away.

8 We pray as in Elisha's case,
  When great Elijah went,
May double portions of thy grace,
  To us who stay be sent.

HYMN 77. P. M.

1 COME, my soul, and let us try,
  For a little season,
Ev'ry burden to lay by,
  Come, and let us reason:

What is this that casts you down?
  Who are those that grieve you?
Speak and let the worst be known,
  Speaking may relieve you.

2 Christ by faith I sometimes see.
    Then it doth relieve me;
  But my sins return again,
    They are they that grieve me;
  Troubled like a restless sea,
    Feeble, faint and fearful;
  Plung'd in sin, a sore disease,
    How can I be cheerful.

3 Think on what your Saviour bore
    In the gloomy garden,
  Sweating blood from every pore,
    To procure thy pardon.
  See him stretch'd upon the wood,
    Bleeding, groaning, crying,
  Suff'ring all the wrath of God,
    Groaning, gasping, dying.

HYMN 78. C. M.

1 COME, humble sinner, in whose breast
    A thousand thoughts revolve;
  Come with your guilt and fear oppress'd,
    And make this last resolve:—

2 "I'll go to Jesus, though my sins
  Have like a mountain rose;
I know his courts, I'll enter in,
  Whatever me oppose.

3 "Prostrate I'll lie before his throne,
  And there my guilt confess:
I'll tell him I'm a wretch undone,
  Without his sov'reign grace.

4 "I'll to my gracious king approach,
  Whose sceptre pardon gives,
Perhaps he may command a touch,
  And then the suppliant lives.

5 "Perhaps he may admit my plea,
  Perhaps he'll hear my prayer,
But if I perish, I will pray,
  And perish only there.

6 "I can't but perish if I go,
  I am resolv'd to try,
For if I stay away, I know
  I must for ever die."

HYMN 79. P. M.

1 FROM Egypt lately fled,
  By the Redeemer's grace!
A rough and thorny path we tread,
  In hopes to see his face.
      Hallelujah,
    We are on our journey home.

2 The flesh dislikes the way,
   But faith approves it well:
This only leads to endless day,
   All others lead to hell.
        Hallelujah,
   We are on our journey home.

3 The promis'd land of peace
   Faith keeps in constant view;
How different from the wilderness,
   We now are passing through.
        Hallelujah,
   We are on our journey home

4 Here often from our eyes,
   Clouds hide the light divine;
There we shall have unclouded skies,
   Our sun will always shine.
        Hallelujah,
   We are on our journey home.

5 Here griefs, and cares, and pains,
   And fears distress us sore;
But there eternal pleasure reigns,
   And we shall weep no more.
        Hallelujah,
   We are on our journry home.

HYMN 80. C. M.

1. IN all my Lord's appointed ways,
   My journey I'll pursue;
Hinder me not, ye much lov'd saints,
   For I must go with you.

2 Through floods and flames, if Jesus leads,
 I'll follow where he goes:
Hinder me not, shall be my cry,
 Through earth and hell oppose.

3 Through duty and through trials too,
 I'll go at his command,
Hinder me not, for I am bound
 To my Immanuel's land.

4 And when my Saviour calls me home,
 Still this my cry shall be,
"Hinder me not, come welcome death,
 I'll gladly go with thee."

HYMN 81. P. M.

Composed by a friend.

Christ the Physician of Souls.

Tune—"Come my soul and let us try."

1 FRIENDS of Jesus come and dwell
 Awhile with Christ your treasure,
Come and let your bosoms swell
 With heaven enrapt'ring pleasure.
Sinners who with folly side,
 Leave your scenes of pleasure,
Come and with your Christ abide,
 He's an endless treasure.

2 Sinners come and know awhile
　　The purest joy of feeling,
　Come receive a Saviour's smile,
　　And prove his power of healing.
　He can calm the soul to rest,
　　Soothe the force of anguish,
　Every one is freely blest,
　　Who for Christ doth languish.

3 Hushed is every inward fear,
　　Every sorrow's banished,
　Silenced every troubling care,
　　Every grief is vanished.
　Joy supreme, within the soul,
　　Knows no bounds to pleasure,
　For the heart without control,
　　Feeds on Christ her treasure.

4 Drink again, my soul of love,
　　Enjoy the sweets of feeling,
　Dwell on Christ, who reigns above,
　　And owns the art of healing;
　Let the heavenly calm of love
　　Be thy choicest treasure;
　Go, my soul, for ever move
　　With Christ in scenes of pleasure.

HYMN 82.　P. M.

HITHER, ye faithful, haste with songs of triumph,
　To Bethlehem go, the Lord of life to meet;

To you this day, is born a Prince and Saviour,
Oh come, and let us worship at his feet.

2 Oh Jesus! for such wond'rous condescension,
Our praise and rev'rence are an off'ring meet;
Now is the word made flesh and dwells among us,
Oh come, and let us worship at his feet.

3 Shout his almighty name, ye choirs of angels,
Let the celestial courts his praise repeat;
Unto our God be glory in the highest,
Oh come and let us worship at his feet.

HYMN 83. P. M.

1 NAY, I cannot let thee go,
'Till a blessing thou bestow;
Do not turn away thy face,
Mine's an urgent, pressing case.

2 Dost thou ask me who I am?
Ah! my Lord, thou know'st my name;
Yet the question gives a plea,
To support my suit with thee.

3 Thou didst once a wretch behold,
In rebellion blindly bold,
Scorn thy grace, thy pow'r defy,
That poor rebel, Lord, was I.

4 Once a sinner, near despair,
Sought thy mercy-seat by pray'r;
Mercy heard, and set him free,
Lord, that mercy came to me.

5 Many years have pass'd since then,
Many changes I have seen;
Yet I've been upheld 'till now,
Who could hold me up but thou?

6 Thou hast help'd in ev'ry need,
This emboldens me to plead;
After so much mercy past,
Canst thou let me sink at last?

7 No, I must maintain my hold,
'Tis thy goodness makes me bold;
I can no denial take,
When I plead for Jesu's sake.

HYMN 84. C. M.

1 MY God was with me all the night,
And gave me sweet repose;
His angels watch'd me while I slept,
Or I had never rose.

2 Now for the mercies of the night,
My humble thanks I'll pay,
And unto God I'll dedicate
The first fruits of the day.

3 In pressing dangers, fears and death,
   Thy goodness I'll adore,
 And praise thee for thy mercies past,
   And humbly hope for more.

4 My life, if thou preserve my life,
   Thy sacrifice shall be;
 And death, when death must be my lot,
   Shall join my soul to thee.

HYMN 85. C. M.

1 GOD counts the sorrows of his saints,
   Their groans affect his ears:
 He has a book for their complaints,
   A bottle for their tears.

2 The Lord can clear the darkest skies,
   Can give us day for night,
 Make drops of sacred sorrow rise
   To rivers of delight.

3 Let those who sow in sadness, wait
   'Till the fair harvest come;
 They shall confess their sheaves are great,
   And shout the blessing home.

HYMN 86. P. M.

1 THE gospel's joyful sound
   Is music in my ears;
 In Jesus I have found
   Relief from all my fears,

Darkness to light does now give place,
And all things wear a different face.

2 Since God is reconcil'd,
    I fear no dire alarms;
He owns me for his child,
    And clasps me in his arms.
Transported with seraphic joy,
I Father, Abba Father, cry.

3 I cannot fear the law,
    Its thunders now may roar,
Since I my Saviour saw,
    They can affright no more.
On wings of love I mount, I fly,
And Father, Abba Father, cry.

4 Death too has lost his sting,
    And wears a smiling face;
I hope to shout and sing,
    Ev'n in his cold embrace.
He'll close my eyes and shut my ears,
But cannot rouse my guilty fears.

5 When through the flaming sky,
    I see the judge descend,
I'll Abba Father cry,
    And hail him as my friend.
While standing in the gospel light,
There's nothing can my soul affright

6 Now let my flowing eyes
   Run down with grateful tears,
Since free adopting grace,
   Has banished all my fears:
And still my sinful self deny,
When I express the heav'n born cry.

7 No more let me return,
   Beneath the galling yoke,
Or e'er embrace those chains,
   Which grace divine has broke.
Let Abba Father be my cry,
In time and in eternity.

HYMN 87. C. M.

1 BEHOLD the wretch, whose lust and wine
   Had wasted his estate,
He begs a share amongst the swine,
   To taste the husks they eat!

2 "I die with hunger here," he cries,
   "I starve in foreign lands;
My father's house has large supplies,
   And bounteous are his hands.

3 "I'll go, and with a mournful tongue,
   Fall down before his face;
Father, I've done thy justice wrong
   Nor can deserve thy grace."

4 He said, and hasten'd to his home,
   To seek his father's love;
The father saw the rebel come,
   And all his bowels move.

5 He ran and fell upon his neck,
   Embrac'd and kiss'd his son;
The rebel's heart with sorrow break
   For follies he had done.

6 "Take off his clothes of shame and sin,"
   The father gives command;
"Dress him in garments white and clean,
   With rings adorn his hand.

7 "A day of feasting I ordain,
   Let mirth and joy abound:
My son was dead, and lives again;
   Was lost, and now is found."

HYMN 88. C. M.

1 YE humble souls, approach your God
   With songs of sacred praise;
For he is good, immensely good,
   And kind are all his ways.

2 All nature owns his guardian care;
   In him we live and move;
But nobler benefits declare
   The wonders of his love.

3 He gave his Son, his only Son,
   To ransom rebel worms;
'Tis here he makes his goodness known
   In its diviner forms.

4 To this dear refuge, Lord, we come,
   'Tis here our hope relies;
  A safe defence, a peaceful home,
   When storms of trouble rise.

5 Thine eye beholds, with kind regard,
   The souls who trust in thee—
  Their humble hope thou wilt reward,
   With bliss divinely free.

6 Great God! to thy almighty love,
   What honours shall we raise?
  Not all the raptur'd songs above
   Can render equal praise.

HYMN 89. P. M.

1 YE virgin souls arise,
   With all the dead awake,
  Unto salvation wise,
   Oil in your vessels take:
  Upstarting at the midnight cry,
  Behold your heavenly bridegroom nigh

2 He comes, he comes, to call
   The nations to his bar,
  And take to glory all
   Who meet for glory are:
  Make ready for your full reward;
  Go forth with joy to meet your Lord.

3 Go, meet him in the sky,
   Your everlasting friend—
  Your head to glorify.
   With all his saints ascend:

Ye pure in heart, obtain the grace
To see, without a veil, his face.

4 Ye that have here received
　The unction from above,
And in his spirit liv'd,
　And thirsted for his love:
Jesus shall claim you for his bride:
Rejoice with all the sanctified.

5 Rejoice in glorious hope
　Of that great day, unknown,
When you shall be caught up
　To stand before his throne;
Called to partake the marriage feast,
And lean on our Immanuel's breast.

6 The everlasting doors
　Shall soon the saints receive,
With seraphs, thrones, and powers,
　In glorious joy to live:
And far from sorrow, pain, and sin,
With God eternally shut in.

7 Then let us wait to hear
　The trumpet's welcome sound,
To see our Lord appear,
　May we be watching found!
Enrob'd in righteousness divine,
In which the bride shall ever shine.

HYMN 90. P. M.

1 DEAREST Jesus, though unseen,
　My believing heart must love thee;

Poor despised Nazarene,
   A true and constant friend I prove thee!
Sinking in thy balmy name,
O how I love my dearest Lamb.

2 Night and day I vent my sigh,
   Languishing to see my Saviour,
With warm heart and wond'ring eye,
   I view my dying Lord for ever:
Here I always would abide,
O this I choose and nought beside.

3 Like the widow'd turtle dove,
   I, dear lovely Lamb, mourn for thee
Pants my soul thy love to prove,
   Crying, O my God restore me,
To thy presence sweet and fair,
O how I long to meet thee there.

4 Every moment seems an age,
   'Till thy presence shall relieve me,
'Till thy grace my woes assuage,
   And thy absence no more grieve me:
Welcome, welcome, bleeding Lamb,
O how thy presence feeds the flame.

5 O'er the hills I see him come,
   Quick as darts and piercing lightning,
Scattered o'er the horrid gloom,
   All thy joys are quick and bright'ning;
Welcome, welcome, bleeding Lamb,
O how I love thy dearest name.

HYMN 91. C. M.

1 YONDER—amazing sight!—I see
　The incarnate Son of God,
Expiring on the accursed tree,
　And welt'ring in his blood.

2 Behold a purple torrent run,
　Down from his hands and head:
The crimson tide puts out the sun;
　His groans awake the dead.

3 The trembling earth, the darken'd sky,
　Proclaim the truth aloud;
And with the amaz'd centurion cry,
　"This is the Son of God."

4 So great, so vast a sacrifice
　May well my hope revive:
If God's own Son thus bleeds and dies,
　The sinner sure may live.

5 O that these cords of love divine,
　Might draw me, Lord, to thee!
Thou hast my heart, it shall be thine—
　Thine it shall ever be!

HYMN 92. P. M.

1 ANGELS, roll the rock away,
Death yield up thy mighty prey:
See! he rises from the tomb,
Glowing with immortal bloom.
　　　　　　　　　　Hallelujah.

2 'Tis the Saviour, angels, raise
 Fame's eternal trump of praise;
 Let the earth's remotest bound
 Hear the joy-inspiring sound.
  Hallelujah.

3 Now, ye saints, lift up your eyes,
 Now to glory see him rise,
 In long triumph up the sky,
 Up to waiting worlds on high.
  Hallelujah.

4 Heav'n displays her portals wide,
 Glorious Saviour, through them ride:
 King of glory, mount thy throne,
 Thy great Father's and thy own.
  Hallelujah

5 Praise him, all ye heav'nly choirs,
 Praise and sweep your golden lyres;
 Shout, O earth, in rapt'rous song,
 Let the strains be sweet and strong.
  Hallelujah.

6 Ev'ry note with wonders swell,
 Sin o'erthrown, and captiv'd hell;
 Where is hell's once dreaded king?
 Where, O death, thy mortal sting?
  Hallelujah.

HYMN 93. C. M.

1 ALL hail the power of Jesu's name!
  Let angels prostrate fall;
 Bring forth the royal diadem,
  To crown him Lord of all.

2 Let high-born seraphs tune the lyre,
  And as they tune it fall
 Before his face who tunes their choir,
  And crown him Lord of all.

3 Crown him, ye morning stars of light,
  He fix'd this floating ball;
 Now hail the strength of Israel's might,
  And crown him Lord of all.

4 Crown him ye martyrs of your God,
  Who from his altar call;
 Extol the stem of Jesse's rod,
  And crown him Lord of all.

5 Ye seed of Israel's chosen race,
  Ye ransom'd of the fall,
 Hail him who saves you by his grace,
  And crown him Lord of all.

6 Hail him, ye heirs of David's line
  Whom David Lord did call;
 The God incarnate, man divine,
  And crown him Lord of all.

7 Sinners! whose love can ne'er forget
    The wormwood and the gall,
  Go—spread your trophies at his feet
    And crown him lord of all.

8 Let ev'ry tribe, and ev'ry tongue,
    That hear the Saviour's call,
  Now shout an universal song,
    And crown him Lord of all.

HYMN 94. C. M

1 DIDST thou, dear Jesus, suffer shame,
    And bear the cross for me?
  And shall I fear to own thy name,
    Or shall I basely flee?

2 Forbid it, Lord that I should dread,
    To suffer shame or loss;
  Oh! let me in thy footsteps tread,
    And glory in thy cross.

3 Inspire my soul with love divine,
    And holy courage bold;
  Let knowledge, faith, and meeknes shine,
    Nor love, nor zeal grow cold.

4 Say to my soul, why dost thou fear
    The face of feeble man?
  Behold thy heav'nly captain's here,
    Before thee in the van.

5 Oh! how my soul would rise and run,
　　At this reviving word;
　Nor any painful suff'rings shun,
　　To follow thee my Lord.

6 Let sinful men reproach, defame,
　　And call me what they will,
　If I may glorify thy name,
　　And be thy servant still.

HYMN 95.　P. M.

1 COME, Holy Ghost, my soul inspire,
　　Bear witness that I'm born again;
　Come, and baptize me, Lord, with fire,
　　Nor let a doubt or cloud remain;
　Give me the sense of sin forgiv'n,
　Sweet foretaste of approaching heav'n.

2 Oh! give the indisputable seal,
　　That ascertains the kingdom mine:
　True holiness I long to feel,
　　The signature of love divine:
　Oh! shed it in my heart abroad,
　Fulness of love, of heav'n, of God!

HYMN 96.　C. M.

1 HARK! from the tombs a doleful sound:
　　My ears attend the cry;
　"Ye living men, come view the ground,
　　Where you must shortly lie.

2 "Princes, this clay must be your bed,
   In spite of all your towers!
 The tall, the wise, the reverend head,
   Must lie as low as ours."

3 Great God! is this our certain doom?
   And are we still secure?
 Still walking downward to the tomb,
   And yet prepare no more?

4 Grant us the power of quick'ning grace,
   To fit our souls to fly:
 Then, when we drop this dying flesh,
   We'll rise above the sky.

HYMN 97. S. M.

1 AND will the judge descend?
   And must the dead arise?
 And not a single soul escape
   His all-discerning eyes?

2 And from his righteous lips
   Shall this dread sentence sound;
 And through the numerous guilty throng,
   Spread black despair around.

3 "Depart from me accurs'd,
   To everlasting flame,
 For rebel angels first prepar'd
   Where mercy never came."

4 How will my heart endure
  The terrors of that day:
When earth and heav'n, before his face,
  Astonish'd shrink away?

5 But ere that trumpet shakes
  The mansions of the dead;
Hark, from the gospel's cheering sound,
  What joyful tidings spread!

6 Ye sinners, seek his grace,
  Whose wrath ye cannot bear;
Fly to the shelter of his cross,
  And find salvation there.

7 So shall that curse remove,
  By which the Saviour bled;
And the last awful day shall pour
  His blessings on your head.

HYMN 98. L. M.

1 COME, gracious Spirit, heav'nly Dove,
With light and comfort from above;
Be thou our guardian, thou our guide,
O'er every thought and step preside.

2 Conduct us safe, conduct us far
From every sin and hurtful snare;
Lead to thy word that rules must give,
And teach us lessons how to live.

3 The light of truth to us display,
And make us know and choose thy way;
Plant holy fear in ev'ry heart,
That we from God may ne'er depart.

4 Lead us to holiness, the road
That we must take to dwell with God:
Lead us to Christ, the living way,
Nor let us from his pastures stray.

5 Lead us to God, our final rest,
In his enjoyment to be bless'd:
Lead us to heav'n, the seat of bliss
Where pleasure in perfection is.

HYMN 99. L M.

1 O MAY I worthy prove to see
The saints in full prosperity;
To see the bright, the glitt'ring bride,
Close seated by her Saviour's side.
Hallelujah.

2 O may I find some humble seat,
Beneath my dear Redeemer's feet;
A servant as before I've been,
And sing salvation to my king.
Hallelujah

3 I'm glad that I am born to die,
From grief and woe my soul shall fly,

Bright angels shall convey me home,
Away to new Jerusalem.
Hallelujah.

4 I'll praise my maker while I've breath,
I hope to praise him after death,
I hope to praise him when I die,
And shout salvation as I fly.
Hallelujah.

5 Farewell, vain world, I'm going home,
My Saviour smiles and bids me come;
Sweet angels beckon me away,
To sing God's praise in endless day.
Hallelnjah.

6 I soon shall pass the veil of death
And in his arms I'll lose my breath;
And then my happy soul shall tell
My Jesus has done all things well.
Hallelujah.

7 I soon shall hear the awful sound,
Awake ye nations under ground:
Arise and drop your dying shrouds,
And meet king Jesus in the clouds.
Hallelujah.

8 When to that blessed world I rise,
And join the anthems in the skies,
This note above the rest shall swell,
My Jesus has done all things well.
Hallelujah.

9 Then shall I see my blessed God,
   And praise him in his bright abode;
   My theme through all eternity
   Shall glory, glory, glory, be.
Hallelujah.

HYMN 100. C. M.

1 MORTALS awake, with angels join,
   And chaunt the solemn lay;
   Joy, love, and gratitude combine,
   To hail the auspicious day.

2 In heav'n the rapt'rous song began,
   While sweet seraphic fire,
   Through all the shining legions ran,
   And tun'd the golden lyre.

3 Swift through the vast expanse it flew,
   And loud the echo roll'd;
   The theme, the song, the joy was new;
   'Twas more than heav'n could hold.

4 Down through the portals of the sky
   The impetuous torrent ran,
   And angels flew with eager joy
   To bear the news to man.

5 Wrapt in the silence of the night
   Lay all the eastern world,
   When bursting, glorious, heav'nly light
   The wondrous scene unfurl'd.

6 Hark! the cherubic armies shout,
　　And glory leads the song:
　Good-will and peace are heard throughout
　　The harmonious, heav'nly throng.

7 Hail prince of life, for ever hail!
　　Redeemer, brother, friend!
　Tho' earth, and time, and life should fail,
　　Thy praise shall never end.

HYMN 101. C. M.

1 WHEN langour and disease invade
　　This trembling house of clay,
　'Tis sweet to look beyond my pains,
　　And long to fly away.

2 Sweet to look inward, and attend
　　The whispers of his love;
　Sweet to look upwards to the place
　　Where Jesus pleads above.

3 Sweet to look back, and see my name
　　In life's fair book set down;
　Sweet to look forward, and behold
　　Eternal joys my own.

4 Sweet to reflect how grace divine
　　My sins on Jesus laid;
　Sweet to remember that his blood
　　My debt of suff'ring paid.

5 Sweet in his righteouness to stand,
   Which saves from second death;
Sweet to experience, day by day,
   His Spirit's quick'ning breath.

6 Sweet in his faithfulness to rest,
   Whose love can never end;
Sweet on his covenant of grace
   For all things to depend.

7 If such the sweetness of the streams,
   What must the fountain be,
Where saints and angels draw their bliss
   Immediately from thee!

HYMN. 102. C. M.

1 SWEET to rejoice in lively hope,
   That when my change shall come,
Angels shall hover round my bed,
   And waft my spirit home.

2 There shall my disembodied soul
   View Jesus and adore;
Be with his likeness satisfy'd,
   And grieve and sin no more.

3 Shall see him wear that very flesh
   On which my guilt was lain;
His love intense, his merit fresh,
   As though but newly slain.

4 Soon too, my slumb'ring dust shall hear
　The trumpet's quick'ning sound;
And, by my Saviour's power rebuilt,
　At his right hand be found.

5 These eyes shall see him in that day,
　The God that died for me;
And all my rising bones shall say,
　Lord, who is like to thee?

6 If such the views which grace unfolds,
　Weak as it is below,
What raptures must the church above
　In Jesu's presence know!

7 O may the unction of these truths
　For ever with me stay;
Till, from her sinful cage dismiss'd,
　My spirit flies away.

HYMN 103. C. M.

1 IN ev'ry trouble sharp and strong
　My soul to Jesus flies;
My anchor-hold is firm in him,
　When swelling billows rise.

2 His comforts bear my spirits up,
　I trust a faithful God,
The sure foundation of my hope,
　Is in a Saviour's blood.

3 Loud hallelujah sing, my soul,
To thy Redeemer's name;
In joy and sorrow, life and death,
His love is still the same.

HYMN 104. P. M.

1 HARK! hark, what sounds are these so pleasing!
Sinners, wipe the falling tear;
'Tis love divine and never ceasing,
Flows from Jesus to the ear.

2 "Come unto me all ye that labour;
Sinners, heavy laden come;"
None are more welcome to the Saviour
Than the wretched and undone.

3 Let not the weight of sin distress you,
Cease to heave the plaintive sigh;
A hearty welcome now awaits you;
"Come, and you shall never die."

4 Come, ye sinners, come and wonder
How such mercy you withstood;
Parch'd with thirst, and starv'd with hunger,
Satiate your souls with good.

5 If by sin and sore temptation,
Heavy laden and opprest,
Behold the gracious invitation,
"Come and I will give you rest."

PART SECOND.

1 NO longer let the tempter keep you
  Fast in chains of unbelief;
Though late in life, the word assures you,
  Christ could save the dying thief.

2 Mary Magdalen too can witness,
  To the mercy she receiv'd:
Then doubt no longer of your fitness—
  Saul, of sinners chief, believ'd.

3 Ho! all ye sinners, heavy laden,
  Fly to Christ, the Saviour's breast;
Receive the pressing invitation,
  "Come, and I will give you rest."

HYMN 105. S. M.

1 THOU God of Jabez, hear,
  While we entreat thy grace,
And borrow that expressive pray'r
  With which he sought thy face.

2 "O that the Lord indeed,
  Would me his servant bless,
From ev'ry evil shield my head,
  And crown my paths with peace.

3 Be his Almighty hand
  My helper and my guide,
'Till, with his saints in Canaan's land
  My portion he divide."

4 Thus pious Jabez pray'd,
   While God inclined his ear;
 And all by whom this suit is made,
   Shall find the blessing near.

5 Ye youths your vows combine,
   With loud united voice;
 So shall your heads with honour shine,
   And all your hearts rejoice.

HYMN 106. C. M.

1 THRO' all the downward tracts of time,
   God's watchful eye surveys;
 O, who so wise to choose our lot,
   Or regulate our ways.

2 I cannot doubt his bounteous love,
   Unmeasurably kind;
 To his unerring, gracious will,
   Be ev'ry wish resign'd.

3 Good when he gives, supremely good,
   Nor less when he denies;
 Ev'n crosses from his sov'reign hand
   Are blessings in disguise.

4 In thy fair book of life divine
   My God, inscribe my name;
 There let me fill some humble place,
   Beneath the slaughter'd Lamb.

HYMN 107. P. M.

1 CAST thy burdens on the Lord,
　　Leave them with thy Saviour;
　He, (whose hands for thee were bor'd,)
　　Can and will deliver.

2 Why should sorrows bow thee down,
　　Trials or temptation!
　Is not Christ, upon the throne,
　　Still thy strong salvation?

3 Roll thy burdens on the Lord,
　　Leave them with thy Saviour;
　He, (whose hands for thee were bor'd,)
　　Can and will deliver.

HYMN 108. P. M.

GUIDE me, O thou great Jehovah,
　Pilgrim through this barren land;
I am weak, but thou art mighty—
　Hold me with thy powerful hand:
　　Bread of heaven,
　Feed me till I want no more,

Open now the chrystal fountain,
　Whence the healing streams do flow:
Let the fiery, cloudy pillar,
　Lead me all my journey through:
　　Strong deliv'rer!
　Be thou still my strength and shield.

3 Feed me with the heav'nly manna,
   In this barren wilderness:
Be my sword, and shield, and banner,
   Be my robe of righteousness:
      Fight and conquer
   All my foes by sov'reign grace.

4 When I tread the verge of Jordan.
   Bid my anxious fears subside;
Foe to death, and hell's destruction,
   Land me safe on Canaan's side,
      Songs of praises
   I will ever give to thee.

HYMN 109 C. M.

1 HOW sweet the name of Jesus sounds
   In a believer's ear!
It sooths his sorrows, heals his wounds,
   And drives away his fear.

2 It makes the wounded spirit whole,
   And calms the troubled breast;
'Tis manna to the hungry soul,
   And to the weary rest.

3 Dear name! the rock on which I build,
   My shield and hiding place;
My never failing treasury, fill'd
   With boundless stores of grace.

4 Jesus! my shepherd, husband, friend,
   My prophet, priest and king;
My Lord, my life. my way, my end,
   Accept the praise I bring.

5 Weak is the effort of my heart,
  And could my warmest thought,
But when I see thee as thou art,
  I'll praise thee as I ought.

6 'Till then I would thy love proclaim,
  With ev'ry fleeting breath:
And may the music of thy name
  Reflesh my soul in death.

HYMN 110. P. M.

1 BEGONE! unbelief, my Saviour is near,
And for my relief will surely appear:
By pray'r let me wrestle, and he will perform,
With Christ in the vessel, I smile at the storm.

2 Tho' dark be my way, since he is my guide,
'Tis mine to obey, 'tis his to provide;
Though cisterns be broken, and creatures all fail.
The word he has spoken will surely prevail.

3 His love in time past forbids me to think
He'll leave me at last in trouble to sink;
Each sweet Ebenezer I have in review,
Confirms his good pleasure to bring me quite through.

4 Since all that I meet shall work for my good,
The bitter is sweet, the med'cine is food;
Though painful at present, 'twill cease before long,
And then, O how pleasant the conqueror's song.

HYMN 111. S. M.

1 MY soul, be on thy guard,
   Ten thousand foes arise;
And hosts of sins are pressing hard,
   To draw thee from the skies.

2 O watch, and fight, and pray,
   The battle ne'er give o'er;
Renew it boldly ev'ry day
   And help divine implore.

3 Ne'er think the vict'ry won,
   Nor once at ease sit down:
Thy arduous work will not be done,
   'Till thou hast got thy crown.

4 Fight on, my soul, till death
   Shall bring thee to thy God;
He'll take thee, at thy parting breath,
   Up to his blest abode.

HYMN 112. C. M.

1 APPROACH, my soul, the mercy-seat,
   Where Jesus answers prayer;
There humbly fall before his feet,
   For none can perish there.

2 Thy promise is my only plea,
   With this I venture nigh:
Thou callest burden'd souls to thee,
   And such, O Lord, am I.

3 Bow'd down beneath a load of sin,
   By Satan sorely prest;
By war without, and fears within,
   I come to thee for rest.

4 Be thou my shield and hiding place,
   That, shelter'd near thy side,
I may my fierce accuser face,
   And tell him "thou hast died."

5 O wonderous love! to bleed and die,
   To bear the cross and shame;
That guilty sinners, such as I,
   Might plead thy gracious name.

6 "Poor tempest-tost soul be still,
   My promis'd grace receive;"
'Tis Jesus speaks, I must, I will,
   I can, I do believe.

HYMN 113. P. M.

The weary Pilgrim's consolation.

1 COME, and taste along with me
    The weary Pilgrim's consolation;
Boundless mercy running free,
    The earnest of complete salvation
Joy and peace in Christ I find,
My heart to him is all resign'd;
The fulness of his power I prove,
And all my soul's dissolved in love.
    Jesus is the Pilgrim's portion,
    Love is boundless as the ocean.

2 When the world of flesh would rise,
    And strive to draw me from my Saviour,
Strangers slight, or friends despise,
    I then more highly prize his favour.
Friends, believe me when I tell,
If Christ be present, all is well:
The world and flesh in vain may rise,
I all their efforts do despise.
    In the world I've tribulation,
    But in Christ I've consolation.

3 Worldlings hold me in disdain,
    Because I shun their carnal pleasure;
All in this which gives me pain
    Is, that they slight a noble treasure.
But still among them, bless the Lord!
There are some who tremble at his word;

And this doth joy to me impart,
To think the Lord hath reach'd their heart.
  O the grace to sinners given,
  Peace on earth, and crowns in heaven.

4 When I'm in the house of prayer.
    I find him with the congregation:
Music sweet unto my ear
    Is the glad sound of free salvation.
When I join to sing his praise,
My heart in holy raptures raise;
I join, and sing, and shout aloud,
And disregard the gazing crowd.
  Glorious theme of exultation,
  What I feel is past expression.

5 When I hear the pleasing sound
    Of weeping mourners just converted,
The dead's alive, the lost is found,
    The Lord hath healed the broken hearted.
My heart exults, my spirits glow,
I love my Lord and brethren so;
Oh had I wings like Noah's dove,
I soon would sing with those above.
  Glory, honour, and salvation,
  What I feel is past expression.

6 Why should I regard the frowns
    Of those who mock, deride, or slight me;
Soon I'll lie beneath the ground,
    Beyond the reach of those who hate me.
Sorrows, toils, and sufferings o'er,
When once we reach that happy shore;

There, with the shining hosts above,
I'll sing and shout redeeming love.
   Blessings there beyond expression,
   Ever roll in sweet succession.

7 Sinners, you may laugh and scorn;
   Your moments lost will be lamented;
The awful day is hastening on,
   When you will wish you had repented.
Death in its embraces cold,
Will soon your mortal bodies hold,
Then all your pleasures take their flight,
And down you'll sink to endless night:
   While you're of that guilty number,
   Your destruction doth not slumber.

8 Fellow sinner go with me,
   My heart's enlarged to receive you;
Slight not mercy offer'd free,
   Come to Jesus he'll relieve you:
But if you offer'd grace refuse,
And will destruction ever choose;
Unhappy souls your guilt and blood,
Will rest on your defenceless head:
   Darkness, torment, pain and sorrow,
   May be yours before to-morrow.

9 Mourner see your Saviour stand,
   With arms expanded to receive you;
He spreads for you his bleeding hands,
   Venture on him, he'll relieve you:
Cast all your doubts and fears aside,
The door of mercy's open wide;

The fountain flows which saves from sin;
Come now believe and enter in.
  Don't distrust your blessed Saviour;
  Come, believe, and live for ever.

HYMN 114. P. M.

1 Vital spark of heav'nly flame,
Quit, oh quit, this mortal frame,
Trembling, hoping, ling'ring, flying,
Oh, the pain, the bliss of dying!
  Cease fond nature, cease thy strife,
  And let me languish into life.

2 Hark! they whisper: angels say,
Sister spirit, come away:
What is this absorbs me quite?
Steals my senses, shuts my sight?
  Drowns my spirit, draws my breath?
  Tell me, my soul, can this be death?

3 The world recedes: it disappears!
Heav'n opens on my eyes! my ears!
  With sounds seraphic ring!
Lend, lend your wings! I mount! I fly!
O grave! where is thy victory?
  O death! where is thy sting?

HYMN 115. C. M.

1 O FOR a breeze of heav'nly love,
  To waft my soul away,
To the celestial world above,
  Where pleasures ne'er decay.

2 Eternal Spirit deign to be,
　My pilot here below,
To steer thro' life's tempestuous sea,
　Where stormy winds doth blow.

3 From rocks of pride on either hand,
　From quicksands of despair;
O guide me safe to Canaan's land,
　Thro' ev'ry latent snare.

4 Anchor me in that port above,
　On that celestial shore,
Where dashing billows never move,
　Where tempests never roar.

HYMN 116. P. M.

1 O ZION, afflicted with wave upon wave,
Whom no man can comfort, whom no man can save,
Surrounded with troubles, with terror dismay'd.
With toiling and rowing thy strength is decay'd.
Loud roaring the billows, now night, thee o'erwhelm,
But skilful the pilot that sits at the helm;
His wisdom conducts thee, his power shall defend,
'Till he, all victorious, thy warfare shall end.

O fearful, O faithless, in mercy he cries,
What though high the surges to affright thee arise;
Still, still I am with thee, my promise shall stand,
Through tossings and tempests I'll bring thee to land.
Forget thee I will not, I care for thy name,
Engrav'd on my heart, it shall ever remain;
The palms of my hands, when I look on I see,
The wounds I receiv'd, when I suffered for thee.

The fearful, the faithless, the weak are my care,
The helpless, the hopeless, I hear their sad prayer;—
Through great tribulation my people I bring,
And when they reach heaven the louder they'll sing.
I feel at my heart, all thy sighs and thy groans,
For thou art most nigh me, my flesh and my bones;
In all thy afflictions, though great is thy pain,
They all are most needful, not one is in vain.

The day of eternal salvation draws near,
When Jesus our leader will dry every tear,
Our bodies and souls shall his glory partake,
When the trumpet shall sound, and the nations awake.

Fight on, ye old soldiers, you'll soon be discharg'd,
The war will be ended, your treasure enlarged,
With singing and shouting, though Jordan may roar;
We'll enter fair Canaan and stand on the shore.

HYMN 117. P. M.

1 WHEN the fierce north wind with his airy forces
Rears up the ocean to a foaming fury,
And the red lightning with a storm of hail come
    Rushing amain down.

2 How the poor sailors stand amaz'd and tremble,
While the hoarse thunder, like a bloody trumpet,
Roars a loud onset to the gaping waters,
    Quick to devour them.

3 Such shall the noise be, and the wild disorder,
If things eternal may be like these earthly;
Such the dire terror when the great archangel
    Shakes the creation.

4 Tears the strong pillars of the vault of heaven,
Breaks up old marble, the repose of princes,
See the graves open, and the bones arising,
    Flames all around them.

5 Hark! the shrill outcries of the guilty wretches!
Lively, bright horror and amazing anguish,
Stare through their eye-lids, while the living worm lies
    Gnawing within them.

6 Thought, like old vultures, pray upon their heart strings,
And the smart twinges when the eye beholds the
Lofty judge frowning, and a flood of vengeance
    Rolling before him.

7 Hopeless immortals, how they scream and shiver,
While devils push them to the pit wide yawning,
Hideous and gloomy to receive them headlong
    Down to the centre.

8 Stop here my fancy, (all away ye horrid
Doleful ideas,) come, arise to Jesus,
How he sits God-like, and the saints around him
    Thron'd, yet adoring

9 O may I sit there, when he comes triumphant,
Dooming the nations; then ascend to glory,
While our hosannahs all along the passage,
    Shout the Redeemer

HYMN 118. P. M.

1 COME, and taste along with me
Consolation running free,
From my father's wealthy throne,
Sweeter than the honey comb.

CHORUS.

*I'll praise God, and you'll praise God,
And we'll all praise God together;
I'll praise the Lord, for the work that he has
    done,
And we'll bless his name for ever.*

2 Why should Christians feast alone!
Two are better far than one;
The more that come with free good will,
Makes the banquet sweeter still.
              I'll praise God, &c.

3 Now I go to heaven's door.
Asking for a little more;
Jesus gives a double share
Calling me his chosen heir.
              I'll praise God, &c.

4 Goodness running like a stream,
Through the new Jerusalem;
By its constant breaking forth,
Sweetens earth and heaven both.
I'll praise God, &c.

5 Saints in glory sing aloud,
For to see an heir of God
Coming in at heaven's door,
Making up the number more.
I'll praise God, &c.

6 Heav'n here and heav'n there,
Comforts flowing every where;
This I boldly can attest,
That my soul has got a taste.
I'll praise God, &c.

7 Now I go rejoiceing home,
From the banquet of perfume;
Gleaning manna on the road,
Dropping from the mount of God.
I'll praise God, &c.

8 O return, ye sons of grace,
Turn and see God's smiling face;
Hark! he calls backsliders home,
Then from him no longer roam.
I'll praise God, &c.

HYMN 119. L M.

1 OH! give me Lord, my sins to mourn,
My sins which have thy body torn;

Give me with broken heart to see,
Thy last tremendous agony.

2 O could I gain the mountain's height,
And gaze upon that wondrous sight;
O that with Salem's daughters, I
Could stand and see my Saviour die.

3 I'd hang around his feet and cry,
Lord save a soul condemn'd to die,
And let a wretch come near thy throne,
To plead the merits of thy Son.

4 Father of mercy! drop thy frown,
And give me shelter in thy Son;
And with my broken heart comply,
O give me Jesus or I die.

5 O Lord, deny me what thou wilt,
If thou wouldst ease me of my guilt;
Good Lord, in mercy hear me cry,
And give me Jesus or I die.

6 O save my soul from gaping hell,
Or else with devils I must dwell;
Oh might I enter, now I'm come;
Lord Jesus save, or I am gone.

HYMN 120. P. M.

1 EXULTING, rejoicing, hail the happy morning,
 The morning on which the Saviour Christ was born;

Angels of mercy who his birth attended,
O bear our loud hosannahs through the sky.

2 Salvation proclaiming to the guilty nations,
He comes in the glory, and in the power of God;
Angels of mercy, who his steps attended,
O bear our loud hosannahs through the sky.

3 Devoted, submissive, on the cross, expiring,
He bows to the mandate of his Father, God;
Angels of pity, who his death attended,
O bear our loud hosannahs through the sky.

4 He rose from the dead, and up to heaven ascended,
And now intercedeth for the sons of men:
Who would not love so gracious a Redeemer;
We hail thee! Prince and Saviour of lost mankind.

HYMN 121. P. M.

FOR CAMP MEETING.

1 THE trump of the Gospel resounds thro' the land,
Repent, for the kingdom of heav'n's at hand!
Awake thou that sleepest, arise from the dead,
And Christ shall enlighten, and raise up thy head.

2 While the rich, poor, wise, simple, the aged and youth,
In the north, south, and west, are embracing the truth—
Bring near, heav'nly Father, to us the glad hour,
The times of refreshing—the day of thy power.

3 With bowels of mercy, O Jesus survey,
The great congregation assembled to-day;
Of names and sects divers—the price of thy blood,
Who long have revolted, and wander'd from God.

4 Let the cloud of thy glory o'ershadow the whole—
A deep veneration impress on each soul—
And strengthen thy servants thy word to proclaim,
And work for the honour and praise of thy name.

5 In copious effusions thy free Spirit shed,
Requicken the living, and quicken the dead!
On penitent sinners thine own image stamp,
And awaken the shout of a king in the camp.

6 Let bigotry fall, Lord, like Dagon of old,
O'erturn Satan's kingdom—thy standard unfold,
And raise up an army thy name to adore,
While life's current flows and when time is no more.

HYMN 122. C. M.

1 WHEN faith presents the Saviour's death,
  And whispers, "this is mine:"
Sweetly my rising hours advance,
  And peacefully decline.

2 Let outward things go how they will,
  On thee I cast my care;
But let me reign with thee in heaven,
  Though most unworthy here.

3 Faith in thy love shall sweeten death,
  And smooth the rugged way;
Smile on me, dearest Lord, and then
  I shall not wish to stay.

HYMN 123. P. M.

1 ON the brink of fiery ruin,
  Justice, with a flaming sword,
Was my guilty soul pursuing,
  When I first beheld my Lord.

2 Terrified with Sinai's thunder,
  Straight I flew to Calvary,
Where I saw with love and wonder,
  Him by faith who died for me.

3 "Sinner," he exclaim'd "I've loved thee
  With an everlasting love;
Justice has in me approv'd thee;
  Thou shalt dwell with me above.

4 Sweet as angels' notes in heaven,
   When to golden harps they sound,
 Is the voice of sins forgiven,
   To the soul by Satan bound.

5 Sweet as angels' harps in glory,
   Was that heavenly voice to me,
 When I saw my Lord before me
   Bleed and die to set me free!

6 Saints attend with holy wonder!
   Sinners, hear and sing his praise:
 'Tis the God that holds the thunder,
   Shows himself the God of grace'

HYMN 124. C. M

Class-Meeting.

1 LORD! when together here we meet,
   And taste thy heav'nly grace,
 Thy smiles are so divinely sweet,
   We're loath to leave the place.

2 Yet, Father, since it is thy will
   That we must part again,
 O let thy gracious presence still
   With ev'ry one remain.

3 Thus let us all in Christ be one,
   Bound with the cords of love,
 'Till we around thy glorious throne
   Shall joyous meet above.

4 Where sin and sorrow from each heart,
   Shall then for ever fly,
And not one thought that we should part,
   Once intercept our joy.

5 Where, void of all distracting pains,
   Our spirits ne'er shall tire:
But in seraphic, heavenly strains,
   Redeeming love admire.

6 And thus, through all eternity,
   Upon the heav'nly shore,
The great mysterious One in Three,
   Jehovah we'll adore.

HYMN 125. P. M.

1 A FEW more days on earth to spend,
And all my toils and cares shall end,
Then I shall see my God and friend,
   And praise his name on high.
There's no more sighs, and no more tears,
There's no more pains, and no more fears,
But God and Christ and heav'n appears,
   Unto the ravish'd eye.

2 Then, oh! my soul, despond no more,
The storm of life will soon be o'er,
And I shall find the peaceful shore,
   Of everlasting rest.

O happy day! O joyful hour,
When freed from earth, my soul shall tow'r,
Beyond the reach of Satan's power,
   To be for ever blest.

3 My soul anticipates the day,
I'd joyfully the call obey,
Which summonses my soul away,
   To seats prepar'd above.
There I shall see my Saviour's face,
And dwell in his belov'd embrace,
And taste the fulness of his grace,
   And sing redeeming love.

4 Though dire afflictions press me sore,
And death's black billows roll before,
Yet still by faith I see the shore,
   Beyond the rolling flood:
The heav'nly Canaan sweet and fair,
Before my ravish'd eyes appear,
And makes me almost think I'm there,
   To yonder bright abode.

5 To earthly cares I'd say farewell,
And triumph over death and hell,
And go where saints and angels dwell,
   To praise the eternal Three.
I'll join with them that's gone before,
Who sing and shout their suff'rings o'er,
Where pain and parting is no more,
   To all eternity.

6 Adieu ye scenes of noise and show,
  And all this region here below,
  Where nought but disappointments grow,
    A better world's in view.
  My Saviour calls! I haste away,
  I would not here for ever stay,
  Hail! ye bright realms of endless day,
    Vain world, once more adieu.

HYMN 126. L. M,

SUNDAY MORNING.

1 GRANT, gracious father, that this day,
    In peace and comfort I may spend.
  Banish all wordly thoughts away,
    And let my prayers to thee ascend.

2 Keep me in thought, in word, and deed,
    From saying and from doing wrong;
  Supply whate'er thou knowest I need,
    And swell, with grateful praise, my tongue.

3 That at its close I may survey,
    Each thought, each word, and action past,
  And conscience, whisp'ring comfort, say,
    "You need not fear, tho' 'twere your last."

4 'Tis thus, oh God! each day I'd spend,
    'Tis thus I would each hour improve,
  And when this transient life shall end,
    Resign myself unto thy love.

HYMN 127. L. M.

ANOTHER.

1 OH thou whose guardian care hath kept
  Us safe from danger whilst we slept,
And now again, our souls hath blest,
  With this, another day of rest.

2 Gather thou in each wand'ring thought
  Nor let it longer rove from thee,
May thy same mercy that hath bought
  Our souls from sin, "still keep them free."

3 Oh let thy love this day direct
  Our wand'ring feet in paths of peace,
From sin and wrath our souls protect,
  And bid each jarring passion cease.

4 May peace and meekness ever dwell
  Within our hearts, may love divine,
With gratitude our bosoms swell,
  And pard'ning mercy seal us thine.

HYMN 128. P. M.

1 GREAT GOD, on thee our trust is stay'd,
For in thy holy word 'tis said,
  Those who on thee rely,
Shall the full measure of thy love,
With ev'ry gracious promise prove,
  And never, never die.

2 That thought shall wake our slumb'ring powers,
And comfort us in those dark hours,
When troubles gather round:
For he who has the promise given,
Will, if our thoughts are fixed on heaven,
A ready help be found.

3 When earth itself shall melt away,
And nature's brightest sun decay;
The moon be turn'd to blood,
He'll bear us up, he's promised more,
He'll land our souls on Canaan's shore,
Above the fiery flood.

HYMN 129. P. M.

1 YOUNG people all attention give,
While I address you in God's name,
You who in sin and folly live,
Come hear the counsel of a friend,
I sought for bliss in glitt'ring toys,
And rang'd the 'luring scenes of vice,
But never found substantial joys
Until I heard my Saviour's voice.

2 He spake my sins at once forgiv'n,
And wash'd my load of guilt away,
He gave me pardon, peace, and heaven,
And thus I found the good old way:

And now with trembling sense I view,
   Huge billows roll beneath your feet,
For death eternal waits for you,
   Who slight the force of gospel truth.

3 Youth, like the spring, will soon be gone,
   By fleeting time, or conqu'ring death;
You morning sun may set at noon,
   And leave you ever in the dark:
Your sparkling eyes and blooming cheeks
   Must wither, like the blasted rose,
The coffin, earth, and winding sheet,
   Will soon your active limbs enclose.

4 Ye heedless ones that wildly stroll,
   The grave must soon become your bed;
Where silence reigns, and vapours roll,
   In solemn silence round your head:
Your friends may pass that lonesome place,
   And with a sigh move slowly on,
Still gazing on the spires of grass,
   With which your graves are overgrown.

5 But O! the soul where vengeance reigns,
   It sinks with groans and ceaseless cries,
It rolls amidst the burning flames
   In endless woe and agone:
There swallow'd up in darkest night,
   Where devils howl, and thunders roar,
To rage in keen despair and guilt,
   When thousand thousand years are o'er.

6 O! fellow youth, this is the state
    Of all who do free grace refuse,
And soon with you 'twill be too late,
    The way of life in Christ to choose:
Come, lay your carnal weapons by,
    No longer fight against your God;
But with my mission now comply,
    And heaven shall be your great reward.

HYMN 130. P. M.

1 Don't you see my Jesus coming,
    Don't you see him in yonder cloud,
With ten thousand angels round him,
    How they do my Jesus crowd:
I'll arise and go and meet him;
    He'll embrace me in his arms;
In the arms of my dear Jesus,
    O there is ten thousand charms.

2 Death shall not destroy my comfort,
    Christ shall guide me through the gloom,
Down he'll send some heav'n y convoy,
    To convey my spirit home:
Jordan's streams shall ne'er o'erflow me,
    While my Saviour's by my side,
Canaan, Canaan, lies before me,
    Rise and cross the swelling tide.

3 See the happy spirits waiting,
    On the banks beyond the stream,
Sweet responses still repeating,
    Jesus, Jesus, is their theme:

See, they whisper! hark! they call me,
   Sister spirit come away,
Lo I come! earth can't contain me
   Hail ye realms of endless day

4 Worlds of light and crowns of glory
   Far above yon azure sky,
Tho' by faith I now explore ye,
   I'll enjoy you soon on high:
Soon I'll gain a full possession,
   Faith and hope shall henceforth cease,
Lost in love's exhaustless ocean,
   Love that sweetest, brightest grace.

5 Swiftly roll ye lingering hours,
   Seraphs lend your glitt'ring wings,
Love absorbs my ransom'd powers,
   Heav'nly sound around me rings:
Worlds above are bright and glorious
   All beneath are dark and void,
Conquest gained, I'll shout victorious
   In the praises of my God.

6 Smiling angels now surround me,
   Troops resplendent fill the skies,
Glory shining all around me,
   While my towering spirit flies:
Jesus clad in dazzling splendour,
   Now methinks appears in view,
Brethren could you see my Jesus,
   You would serve and love him too.

HYMN 131. P. M.

1 STOP, poor sinners, and look yonder,
  See your sins like mountains rise,
O astonishing the number,
  Higher mounting than the skies:
    Cry for mercy,
Dread the death that never dies.

2 On the crumbling banks of ruin,
  How can you securely dwell?
Sinners, vengeance is pursuing,
  And will sweep you down to hell:
    Then to heaven,
Finally you'll bid farewell.

3 Doom'd where sorrows behind sorrows,
  Follow on without control,
Floods of vengeance big with horror,
  Without intermission roll;
    Wrath vindictive
Overwhelms the guilty soul.

4 Wrapt in sheets of black damnation.
  There the curling flames surround,
Torments endless, no cessation,
  Mercy there cannot be found:
    Dismal yellings, and
In those lower regions bound.

5 See yon sun how swift he hasteth
  Through the circuit of the skies;
How your golden moments wasteth,
  Sinners pray at length be wise:
    O! he's setting,
And may set no more to rise.

6 See how fast your time is flying
  Will ye sinners yet delay?
One is gone, another's dying,
  O! to God for mercy pray:
    Time is precious:
God may next call you away.

7 Now's the time for preparation,
  While the vital air you breathe;
God is offering you salvation,
  Calls you yet to turn and live:
    Boundless mercy;
All who comes he will receive.

8 See the precious blood of Jesus,
  Streaming from the cursed tree,
Will not this suffice to grieve us,
  Jesus spilt his blood for me:
    Come then sinners,
And his great salvation see.

HYMN 132. C. M.

1 THE souls that would to Jesus press
  Must fix this firm and sure,
That tribulations, more or less,
  They must and shall endure.

2 From this there's none can be exempt,
  'Tis God's own wise decree;
Satan the weakest saint will tempt,
  Nor are the strongest free.

3 The world opposes from without,
   And unbelief within,
We fear, we faint, we grieve, we doubt,
   And feel the load of sin.

4 Glad frames too often lift us up,
   And then how proud we grow;
'Till sad desertion makes us droop,
   And down we sink as low.

5 Ten thousand baits the foe prepares
   To catch the wand'ring heart,
And seldom do we see the snares
   Before we feel the smart.

6 But let not all this terrify,
   Pursue the narrow path;
Look to the Lord with steadfast eye,
   And fight with hell by faith.

7 Tho' we are feeble, Christ is strong,
   His promises are true;
We shall be conqu'rers all ere long,
   And more than conqu'rers too.

HYMN 133. C. M.

1 SWEET muse descend, and bless the shade,
   And bless the ev'ning grove!
Business and noise, and day are fled,
   And every care but love.

2 'Tis no mean beauty of the ground,
   That hath enslav'd my eyes;
I faint beneath a nobler wound,
   Nor love below the skies.

3 Jesus has all my pow'rs possess'd,
   My hopes, my fears, my joys:
He, the dear sov'reign of my breast,
   Shall still command my voice.

4 Some of the fairest choirs above,
   Shall flock around my song,
With joy to hear the name they love
   Sound from a mortal tongue.

5 His charms shall make my numbers flow;
   And hold the falling flood,
While silence sits on every bough,
   And bends the list'ning wood.

6 I'll carve thy passion on the bark,
   And ev'ry wounded tree,
Shall droop, and bear some mystic mark,
   That Jesus died for me.

7 The swains shall wonder when they read,
   Inscrib'd on all the grove,
That heav'n itself came down and bled,
   To win a mortal's love.

HYMN 134. P. M.

1 IT grieves me, Lord, it grieves me sore,
That I have liv'd to thee no more,
   And wasted half my days;

My inward pow'r shall burn and flame,
With zeal and passion for thy name;
I could not speak but for my God,
   Nor move but to his praise

2 What are my eyes, but aids to see
The glories of the Deity,
   Inscrib'd with beams of light;
In flow'rs and stars, Lord I behold,
The shining azure green and gold,
But when I try to read thy name,
   A dimness veils my sight.

3 Mine ears are rais'd when Virgil sings,
Sicilian swains, and Trojan kings,
   And drink the music in,
Why should the trumpet's brazen voice,
Or oaten reed awake my joys,
And yet my heart so stupid lie,
   When sacred hymns begin.

4 Change me, O God! my flesh shall be
An instrument of song to thee,
   And now the notes inspire;
My tongue shall keep the heav'nly chime,
My cheerful pulse shall beat the time,
And sweet variety of sound,
   Shall in thy praise conspire.

5 The dearest nerve about my heart
Should it refuse to bear a part,
   With my melodious breath,

I'd tear away the vital chord,
A bloody victim to my Lord,
And live without that impious string,
 Or show my zeal in death.

HYMN 135. P. M.

On Death.

1 HOW dreadful is the thought of death,
That soon will rob us of our breath,
 Though careless some remain;
In glory Christ you'll never see,
Remember sinner this from me,
 You'll feel eternal pain.

2 Soon will your day of grace be o'er,
Its loss for ever you'll deplore,
 Come, now its in thy power,
O! fly to the Redeemer's breast,
On which you may securely rest,
 In death's uncertain hour.

3 When death our bodies shall assail,
Our stronger passions then will fail,
 It sinks us to the grave;
Riches shall then be no defence,
Nor all the powers of eloquence,
 Jesus alone can save.

4 No more let us in sin delight,
But all our days against it fight,
 And when we come to die,

In Christ a lively faith we'll have,
Which reaches far beyond the grave,
And bids us death defy.

5 The righteous soon will meet above,
And prove the Saviour's boundless love;
O! may we with them join;
In concert with the heav'nly host,
Praise Father; Son, and Holy Ghost,
In ecstacies divine.

HYMN 137. L. M.

Another.

1 SOON will this mortal life be o'er,
The body moulder into dust;
Naked my soul will stand before
A God that's holy, pure and just.

2 Its standing doom of bliss or woe
Will from the great I AM receive,
Up to the realms of glory go,
Or in hell's torments ever live.

3 Without an interest in the blood
Of Jesus, shed on Calvary,
We can't escape his vengeful rod,
How e'er so moral here we be,

4 Away then all self-righteousness,
My soul from nature's sleep arise,
Be justified by faith, through grace,
And claim a mansion in the skies.

5 Perfection's height may I ascend,
 And feel my soul dissolv'd in love;
That when my days below shall end,
 Angels may waft my soul above.

HYMN 137. P. M.

1 O HEARKEN sinners, we have cause
 To warn you of your danger,
We pray be reconcil'd to him
 Who once lay in a manger.

CHORUS.

Ho! every one that thirsts,
 Come ye to the waters,
Freely drink and quench your thirst,
 Ye Zion's sons and daughters.

2 The awful God who made your soul,
 And all the world around you,
Doth charge you with ten thousand crimes,
 But hateth to confound you.
     Ho! every one, &c.

3 O seek the circumcising grace,
 Be wise, do not refuse it,
For if you seek your life to save,
 You will be sure to lose it.
     Ho! every one, &c.

4 The cross of Christ you have to bear,
   Fearless of persecution,
  Or groan you will, when time shall cease,
   In darkness and confusion.
               Ho! every one, &c.

5 Come all ye humble, weeping souls,
   Who long to be forgiv'n,
  We bring glad tidings unto you,
   From the good Lord of heav'n.
               Ho! every one, &c.

6 There is a fountain deep and wide,
   For sin and all uncleanness,
  Come drink and wash, and be made white,
   And prove the gospel fulness.
               Ho! every one, &c.

7 Oh! see the crowd that's trav'ling on,
   In paths of self-denial,
  They march along the banks of love,
   And long for your arrival.
               Ho! every one, &c.

8 Shall unbelief debar you from
   The knowledge of your Saviour,
  Believe and you'll be justified,
   Believe and live for ever.
               Ho! every one, &c.

9 I'm not surpris'd that saints do sing,
   Or angels shout and wonder,
  I would sing glory if I could,
   As loud as mighty thunder.
               Ho! every one, &c.

10 My night of sin and grief is gone,
   My soul is fill'd with glory,
 Oh! for a thousand tongues to tell
   Love's animating story.
              Ho! every one, &c.

11 Let heav'n and earth with me unite,
   And sing and shout hosannah,
 The Lord has pardon'd all my sins,
   And fill'd my soul with manna.
              Ho! every one, &c.

12 Poor sinners often laugh and scoff,
   Because I sing hosannah,
 But they don't know what this doth mean
   My soul is eating manna.
              Ho! every one, &c.

13 My old companions think I'm lost
   Because I sing hosannah,
 But they would sing as loud as me,
   If they had tasted manna.
              Ho! every one, &c.

14 The cold proffessors do detest
   Such loud noise and hosannahs;
 And so did we before we sought,
   And found his holy manna.
              Ho! every one, &c.

15 When on my dying bed I lay,
   My soul shall sing hosannah,
 With happy saints that shout around,
   We'll have a feast of manna.
              Ho! every one, &c

16 A glorious throng have gone before,
　　Who sing and shout hosannah,
　They stand around the tree of life,
　　And always gather manna.
　　　　　　Ho! every one, &c.

17 Come on ye follow'rs of the lamb,
　　Love God and sing hosannah,
　We soon shall join that holy throng,
　　And always live on manna.
　　　　　　Ho! every one, &c.

HYMN 138. P. M.

The wheat and tares.

1 THO' in the outward church below
　The wheat and tares together grow;
　Jesus e'er long will weed the crop,
　And pluck the tares in anger up:
　　　For soon the reaping time will come,
　　　And angels shout the harvest home.

2 Will it relieve their horrors there,
　To recollect their stations here,
　How much they heard, how much they knew,
　How much among the wheat they grew?
　　　For soon the reaping time, &c.

3 Oh! this will aggravate their case,
　They perish'd under means of grace;
　To them the word of life and faith
　Became an instrument of death.
　　　　　　And soon, &c.

4 We seem alike when thus we meet,
  Strangers might think we all were wheat;
  But to the Lord's all searching eyes
  Each heart appears without disguise.
                    And soon, &c.

5 The tares are spar'd for various ends;
  Some for the sake of praying friends;
  Others the Lord, against their will,
  Employs his counsels to fulfil.
                    But soon, &c.

6 But tho' they grow so tall and strong,
  His plan will not require them long;
  In harvest when he saves his own,
  The tares shall into hell be thrown.
                    For soon, &c.

7 Most awful thought, and is it so,
  Must all mankind the harvest know?
  Is every man a wheat or tare?
  Me for that harvest, Lord prepare.
              For soon the reaping time, &c.

HYMN 139. P. M.

ROCK OF SALVATION.

1 If life's pleasures charm thee, give them not
        thy heart,
  Lest the gift insnare thee, from thy God to
        part;

His favour seek, his praises speak,
　Fix here thy hope's foundation;
Serve him, and he will ever be,
　The Rock of thy Salvation.

2 If distress befall thee, painful tho' it be,
　Let not grief appal thee, to thy Saviour flee;
　　He ever near, thy prayer will hear,
　　　And calm thy perturbation;
　The waves of woe, shall ne'er o'er flow,
　　The Rock of thy Salvation.

3 When earth's prospects fail thee, let it not distress,
　Better comforts wait thee, Christ will freely bless;
　　To Jesus flee, thy prop he'll be,
　　　Thy heavenly consolation;
　For griefs below cannot o'erthrow,
　　The Rock of thy Salvation.

4 Dangers may approach thee, let them not alarm,
　Christ will ever watch thee, and protect from harm;
　　He near thee stands, with mighty hands,
　　　To ward off each temptation;
　To Jesus fly, he's ever nigh,
　　The Rock of thy Salvation.

5 Let not death alarm thee, shrink not from his blow,
　For thy God shall arm thee, and victory bestow;

For death shall bring, to thee no sting,
  The grave no desolation;
'Tis gain to die, with Jesus nigh,
  The Rock of thy Salvation.

HYMN 141. P. M.

1 GREAT Redeemer, friend of sinners,
   Thou hast wond'rous power to save;
 Grant me grace, and still protect me,
   Over life's tempestuous wave:
 May my soul with sacred transport,
   View the dawn while yet afar,
 And until the sun arises,
   Lead me by the morning star.

2 O! what madness! O! what folly,
   That my heart should go astray;
 After vain and foolish trifles,
   Trifles only of a day:
 This vain world with all its pleasures,
   Very soon will be no more;
 There's no object worth admiring,
   But the God whom we adore.

3 See the happy spirits waiting,
   On the banks beyond the stream,
 Sweet responders still repeating,
   Jesus, Jesus is their theme:
 Hark! they whisper, lo! they call me,
   Sister spirit come away;
 Lo! I come, earth can't contain me,
   Hail the realms of endless day.

4 Swiftly roll ye ling'ring hours,
   Seraphs lend your glitt'ring wings;
Love absolves my ransom powers,
   Heavenly sounds around me rings,
Worlds of light and crowns of glory,
   Far above yon azure sky;
When by faith I now behold you.
   I'll enjoy you soon on high.

HYMN 142. S. M.

The Female Pilgrim.

1 WHITHER go'st thou, Pilgrim, stranger,
   Passing through this darksome vale?
Know'st thou not, 'tis full of danger,
   And will not thy courage fail?
     I'm bound for the kingdom,
     Will you go to glory with me.
        Hallelujah, hallelujah.

2 PILGRIM, thou dost justly call me,
   Wandering o'er this waste so wide;
Yet no harm will e'er befal me,
   While I'm blest with such a GUIDE.
        I'm bound, &c.

3 Such a Guide!—No guide attends thee,
   Hence for thee my fears arise;
If a guardian power befriend thee,
   'Tis unseen by mortal eyes.
        I'm bound, &c.

4 Yes, unseen—but still, believe me,
   Such a Guide my steps attends ;
He'll in every strait relieve me,
   He from every harm defends.
              I'm bound, &c.

5 Pilgrim! see that stream before thee,
   Darkly winding through the vale;
Should its deadly waves roll o'er thee,
   Would not then thy courage fail?
              I'm bound, &c.

6 No: that stream has nothing frightful,
   To its brink my steps I bend,
There to plunge will be delightful—
   There my pilgrimage will end.
              I'm bound, &c.

7 While I gaz'd—with speed surprising
   Down the stream she plung'd from sight;
Gazing still, I saw her rising,
   Like an angel, cloth'd with light.
              I'm bound, &c.

HYMN 143.   P. M.

Gloom of autumn.

1 HAIL, ye sighing sons of sorrow,
   Learn with me your certain doom
Learn with me your fate to-morrow,
   Dead, perhaps laid in the tomb.

See all nature fading, dying,
  Silent all things seem to mourn,
Life from vegetation flying,
  Calls to mind the moulding urn.

2 Lo! in yonder forest standing,
  Lofty cedars how they nod,
Scenes of nature, how surprising;
  Read in nature, nature's God.
While the annual frosts are cropping
  Leaves and tendrils from the trees,
So our friends are yearly dropping
  We are like to one of these.

3 Hollow winds about me roaring,
  Noisy waters round me rise,
While I sit my fate deploring,
  Tears fast streaming from my eyes.
What to me is autumn's treasure,
  Since I know no earthly joy,
Long have I lost all youthful pleasure,
  Time will health and youth destroy.

4 Former friends, how oft I've sought them,
  Just to cheer a troubled mind,
Now they're gone like leaves of autumn,
  Driven before the dreary wind.
When a few more days are wasted,
  And a few more scenes are o'er,
When a few more griefs I've tasted,
  I shall rise to fall no more.

5 Fast my sun of life's declining,
   Soon 'twill set in endless night,
But my hopes pure and reviving,
   Rise to fairer worlds of light.
Cease this trembling, mourning, sighing,
   Death shall burst this sullen gloom,
Then my spirit, fluttering, flying,
   Shall be borne beyond the tomb.

HYMN 144. P. M.

1 As near to Calvary I pass,
  Methinks I see a bloody cross,
    Where a poor victim hangs;
His flesh with rugged irons tore,
His limbs all dress'd in purple gore,
    Gasping in dying pangs.

2 Surpris'd the spectacle to see,
I ask'd, who can this victim be,
    In such exquisite pain?
Why thus consign'd to woes, I cried,
"'Tis I," the bleeding God reply'd,
    "To save a world from sin."

3 A God for rebel mortals dies!
How can it be! my soul replies,
    What! Jesus die for me!
"Yes," saith the suff'ring Son of God,
"I give my life, I spill my blood,
    "For thee, poor soul, for thee."

4 Lord, since thy life thou'st freely giv'n,
To bring my wretched soul to heaven,
And bless me with thy love;
Then at thy feet, O God, I'll fall,
Give thee my life, my soul, my all,
To reign with thee above.

HYMN 145. P. M.

1 See the eternal Judge descending,
Seated on his father's throne;
Now poor sinner, Christ will shew thee
That he's with the Father one:
Trumpet's call thee,
Stand and hear thy awful doom.

2 Hear the sinner now lamenting,
At the sight of fiercer pain;
Cries and tears he now is venting,
But he weeps and cries in vain:
Greatly mourning,
That he ne'er was born again.

3 Yonder sits my slighted Saviour,
With the marks of dying love:
O! that I had sought his favour,
When I felt his spirit move!
Doomed I'm justly,
For I have against him strove.

4 All his wooing I have slighted,
While he daily sought my soul,
If my vows to him I plighted

Yet for sin I broke them all:
Golden moments,
How neglected did they roll!

5 There I see my godly neighbours,
Who were once despis'd by me,
Now they're clad in dazzling splendour,
Waiting my sad fate to see:
Farewell neighbours—
Dismal gulph I'm bound for thee.

6 Hail! ye ghosts that dwell in darkness,
Groaning, rattling, of your chains!
Christ has now denounc'd my sentence,
I'm to dwell in endless pains;
Down I'm rolling,
Never to return again.

7 Now experience plainly shews me,
Hell is not a fabled thing,
Now I see my friends in glory,
Round the throne they ever sing,
I'm tormented
With an everlasting sting.

HYMN 146. P. M.

The benefit of Prayer.

1 WHAT various hindrances we meet,
In coming to the mercy seat;
Yet who that knows the worth of prayer,
But wishes to be often there.

2 Prayer makes the darkest clouds withdraw,
Prayer climbs the ladder Jacob saw,
Gives exercise to faith and love,
Brings ev'ry blessing from above.

3 Restraining prayer, we cease to fight,
Prayer makes the Christian's armour bright,
And Satan trembles when he sees
The weakest saint upon his knees.

4 When Moses stood with arms spread wide,
Success was found on Israel's side:
But when through weariness they fail'd,
That moment Amalek prevail'd.

5 Have you no words? Ah, think again,
Words flow apace when you complain,
And fill your fellow creatures' ear
With the sad tale of all your care.

6 Were half the time that's vainly spent,
To heaven in supplications sent:
Our cheerful songs would oftener be,
Hear what the Lord has done for me.

HYMN 148. C. M.

For a believer in worldly business.

1 LO I come, with joy to do
My master's blessed will;
Him in outward things pursue,
And serve his pleasure still;

Faithful to my Lord's commands,
  I still would choose the better part,
Serve with careful Martha's hands,
  And humble Mary's heart.

2 Careful without care I am,
  Nor feel my happy toil;
Kept in peace by Jesu's name,
  Supported by his smile.
Joyful thus my faith to shew,
  I find his service my reward;
Every work I do below,
  I do it to the Lord.

3 Thou O Lord in tender love;
  Dost all my burdens bear;
Lift my heart to things above,
  And keep it ever there.
Calm on tumult's wheel I sit,
  'Midst busy multitudes, alone;
Sweetly waiting at thy feet,
  Till all thy will be done.

4 To the desert or the cell,
  Let others blindly fly;
In this evil world I dwell,
  Unhurt, unspotted I.
Here I find an house of prayer,
  To which I inwardly retire;
Walking unconcern'd in care,
  And unconsum'd in fire.

5 Thou, O Lord my portion art,
Before I hence remove;
Now my treasure and my heart,
Are all laid up above.
Far above these earthly things,
While yet my hands are here employ'd,
Sees my soul the King of kings,
And freely talks with God.

6 O that all the earth might know,
Of living thus to thee,
Find their heaven begun below,
And here thy goodness see.
Walk in all thy works prepar'd,
By thee to exercise thy grace,
Till they gain their full reward,
And see thy glorious face.

HYMN 149. C. M.

At the funeral of a young person.

1 WHEN blooming youth is snatch'd away
By death's resistless hand,
Our hearts the mournful tribute pay;
Which pity must demand;

2 While pity prompts the rising sigh,
O may this truth, imprest
With awful power,—'I too must die!'
Sink deep in every breast.

17 *

3 Let this vain world engage no more;
   Behold the gaping tomb!
It bids us seize the present hour,
   To-morrow death may come.

4 The voice of this alarming scene,
   May every heart obey;
Nor be the heavenly warning vain,
   Which calls to watch and pray.

5 O let us fly, to Jesus fly,
   Whose powerful arm can save;
Then shall our hopes ascend on high,
   And triumph o'er the grave.

6 Great God, thy sovereign grace impart,
   With cleansing, healing power;
This only can prepare the heart,
   For death's all solemn hour.

HYMN 140. P. M.

1 LORD, and am I yet alive,
Not in torments, not in hell,
Still doth thy good Spirit strive—
With the chief of sinners dwell!
   Tell it, unto sinners tell,
   I am, I am out of hell.

2 Yes, I still lift up mine eyes,
Will not of thy love despair:
Still, in spite of sin, I rise,
Still I bow to thee in pray'r.
   Tell it, &c.

3 O the length and breadth of love:
Jesus, Saviour, can it be?
All thy mercy's height I prove,
All the depth is seen in me.
Tell it, &c.

4 See a bush that burns with fire,
Unconsum'd amid the flame!
Turn aside the sight t' admire—
I the living wonder am!
Tell it &c.

5 See a stone that hangs in air!
See a spark in ocean live!
Kept alive with death so near,
I to God the glory give:
*Ever tell—to sinners tell,
I am, I am out of hell.*

HYMN 151. L. M.

1 WHILE on the verge of life I stand,
And view the scene on either hand,
My spirit struggles with my clay,
And longs to wing its flight away.

2 Where Jesus dwells my soul would be,
And faints my much-lov'd Lord to see:
Earth, twine no more about to my heart,
For 'tis far better to depart.

3 Come, ye angelic convoys, come,
And lead the willing pilgrims home!
Ye know the way to Jesu's throne.
Source of my joys, and of your own!

4 That blissful interview, how sweet
To fall transported, at his feet!
Rais'd in his arms to view his face,
Thro' the full beaming of his grace.

5 As with the seraph's voice to sing,
To fly as on a cherub's wing!
Performing with unweary'd hands,
The present Saviour's high commands.

6 Yet, with these prospects full in sight,
We'll wait the signal for the flight;
For while thy service we pursue,
We find a heav'n in all we do.

HYMN 152. S. M.

1 O WHY should unbelief
Stay the Almighty's hand,
That hand which holds my sure relief,
Though earth and hell withstand.

2 My soul, believe and pray,
Without a doubt believe,
Whate'er we ask in God's own way,
We shall in truth receive.

3 Here stands the promise fair,
   For God cannot repent;
To fervent persevering pray'r,
   He'll every blessing grant.

HYMN 153. S. M.

Believers Sufferings.

1 HOW firm a foundation, ye saints of the Lord
Is laid for your faith in his excellent word,
What more can he say than to you he hath said
You, who unto Jesus for refuge have fled.

2 In every condition, in sickness in health,
In poverty's vail, or abounding in wealth;
At home and abroad, in the land, on the sea,
'As thy days may demand, shall thy strength ever be.

3 Fear not, I am with thee, O be not dismay'd,
'I, I am thy God, and will still give thee aid;
'I'll strengthen thee, help thee and cause thee to stand,
'Upheld by my righteous omnipotent hand.

4 When through the deep waters I call thee to go,
'The rivers of woe shall not thee overflow;
'For I will be with thee, thy troubles to bless,
'And sanctify to thee thy deepest distress.

5 'When through fiery trials thy path way shall lie,
 'My grace all sufficient shall be thy supply,
 'The flame shal. not hurt thee, I only design
 'Thy dross to consume, and thy gold to refine,

6 'Even down to old age, all my people shall prove,
 'My soverign, eternal, unchangeable love;
 'And when hoary hairs shall these temples adorn,
 'Like lambs they shall still in thy bosom be borne.

7 'The soul that on Jesus hath leaned for repose
 'I will not, I will not; desert to his foes,
 'That soul, though all hell should endeavour to shake,
 'I'll never, no never, no never forsake.'

HYMN 153. L. M.

1 WHEN I survey the wond'rous cross
  On which the Prince of Glory dy'd,
 My richest gain I count but loss,
  And pour contempt on all my pride?
 Forbid it, Lord, that I should boast,
  Save in the death of Christ, my God:
 All the vain things that charm me most,
  I sacrifice them to thy blood.

2 See from his head, his hands, his feet,
  Sorrow and love flow mingled down:
 Did e'er such love and sorrow meet,
  Or thorns compose so rich a crown?

Were the whole realm of nature mine,
  That were a present far too small:
Love so amazing, so divine,
  Demands my soul, my life, my all.

HYMN 154. C. M.

1 JESUS, I love thy charming name,
    'Tis music to my ear;
  Fain would I sound it out so loud
    That earth and heav'n might hear,
  Yes thou art precious to my soul,
    My transport and my trust,
  Jewels to thee are gaudy toys;
    And gold is sordid dust.

> *Chor.—A Saviour! let creation sing!*
> *A Saviour! let all heaven ring!*
> *He's God with us, we feel him ours.*
> *His fulness in our souls he pours,*
> *'Tis almost done—'tis almost o'er,*
> *We're joining them who're gone before,*
> *We then shall meet to part no more.*

2 O may thy grace still cheer my heart?
    And shed its fragrance there!
  The noblest balm of all its wounds,
    The cordial of its care.
  I'll speak the honours of thy name,
    With my last lab'ring breath;
  When speechless, clasp thee in my arms:
    My joy in life and death.
                    A Saviour, &c.

HYMN 155. L. M.

1 SHEW me the souls to doubt expos'd,
To such this question is propos'd:
Ask saith the Lord, and let me know,
What I shall now on thee bestow.

2 Say, what thy wants, and what thy woes!
Dost thou in me thy trust repose!
Art thou my friend sincerely true?
Speak, for thy springs of thought I view.

3 Art thou to seriousness inclin'd,
Ask, and I'll solemnize thy mind?
Dost thou want love to Jesus' name!
Ask, and his matchless love proclaim.

4 Dost thou want peace and pardon seal'd.
Ask, for they wait to be reveal'd?
Dost thou want faith and holy fear,
Ask, and behold the blessings near.

5 Dost thou want strength 'gainst sin to fight,
Ask, and I'll make thee strong in might:
Dost thou want light and life divine?
Ask, and eternal life is thine.

6 Wilt thou be made completely whole?
Ask, and I'll renovate thy soul:
This instant ask, arise and pray,
Nor lose such blessings by delay.

HYMN 156. P. M.

Fleeting moments.

1. I'll sing my Saviour's grace,
And his dear name I'll praise.

While in this land of sorrow I remain;
    My troubles soon will end,
    And my soul ascend,
When freed from this dull clod of cumb'rous clay.

2   A pilgrim here below,
    While in this vale of woe,
I live in exile, mourning like the dove;
    My days in sorrow roll,
    And my weary soul,
With earnest longings pants to mount above.

3   Tho' few my days have been,
    Much trouble I have seen,
And deep afflictions I have waded through;
    For thorny is the way,
    To eternal day,
Yet forward will I press, and onward go.

4   Another day is gone,
    And yon declining sun,
Has veil'd his radiant beams in sable shades,
    While gloomy darkness reigns,
    O'er the extensive plains,
And awful silence close the solemn scene.

5   Thus rapid flies away,
    Ev'ry succeeding day,
And life's declining light draws to a close;
    This life's short setting sun,
    Will in death go down,
And lay my weary limbs in sweet repose.

6   On eagle's wings of love,
      Then I'll mount above,
And find my passage safe to endless day;
      Then happy sweet surprise;
      What great new wonders rise,
When freed from this dull clod of cumb'rous clay.

7   O what a glorious sight,
      And what supreme delight,
Will strike my raptur'd soul when I behold—
      Fair Salem's gates I see,
      Open fly to me,
And streets of glitt'ring new transparent gold.

8   But oh! and shall I then,
      Behold the friend of men,
The man who suffer'd, bled, and dy'd for me;
      Who bore my load of sin,
      Sorrow, grief, and pain,
To make me happy, and to set me free?

9   To living fountains then,
      And to rich pastures green,
To trees of paradise he leads his lambs;
      While millions falling down;
      Prostrate all around,
And at his footstool cast their glitt'ring crowns.

10   Ye heav'nly arches ring,
      Sing Hallelujah, sing,
Hail! holy, holy, holy, bleeding lamb;
      Once I was dead in sin,
      But now I live again,
And glory, glory, glory to his name.

INDEX.

A.
	Page
Almighty love inspire my heart, &c.	18
Awak'd by Sinia's awful sound	58
Awake! O guilty world, awake!	80
Arise and shine, O Zion fair	84
Attend, young friends while I relate	92
Arise, and hail the sacred day	88
Afflictions tho' they seen severe	111
Angels roll the rock away	135
All hail the power of Jesu's name!	137
And will the judge descend	140
Approach, my soul, the mercy seat,	155
A few more days on earth to spend,	171
As near to Calvary I pass'd	196

B.
Bright scenes of glory strike my sense,	16
Burst, ye emerald gates and bring	40
Brethren, we have met to worship	75
Behold the wretch whose lust and wine	130
Begone! unbelief, my Saviour is near,	158

C.
Come ye that love the Lord indeed,	22
Come, and taste along with me,	41
Come, all ye weary travellers,	68
Come saints and sinners, hear me tell	71
Come, my soul thy suit prepare,	100
Come, my soul, and let us try,	120
Come humble sinner in whose breast,	121
Come, Holy Ghost, my soul inspire,	139

	Page.
Come, gracious Spirit, heavenly Dove,	141
Cast thy burdens on the Lord,	151
Come, and taste along with me,	156
Come and taste along with me,	164

✦ D.

Don't you see my Jesus coming?	30
Dark and thorny is the desert,	61
Dearest Jesus, tho' unseen,	133
Didst thou dear Jesus suffer shame	138
Don't you see my Jesus coming	177

E.

Exulting, rejoicing, hail the happy morning	166

F.

From the regions of love, &c.	14
From all that's mortal, all that's vain,	56
Farewell, dear friends, I must be gone,	55
Far above yon glorious ceiling	73
Farewell, my dear brethren, the time is at hand	97
Farewell, my dear brethren I bid you farewell,	99
From whence does the union arise,	113
From Egypt lately fled	122
Friends of Jesus come and dwell	124

G.

God counts the sorrows of his saints,	128
Guide me, O thou great Jehovah	151
Grant, gracious Father that this day,	173
Great God on thee our trust is stay'd	174
Great Redeemer, friend of sinners	192

H.

How happy every child of grace,	9

	Page
How lost was my condition,	20
Hail, sovereign love, that first began,	24
Hark! the jubilee is sounding;	74
Hark! my soul, it is the Lord,	96
How sweet, how heavenly is the sight,	101
Hither, ye faithful, haste with songs of triumph	125
Hark! from the tombs a doleful sound	139
Hark! hark! what sounds are these so pleasing	148
How dreadful is the thought of death,	184
Hail ye sighing sons of sorrow	194
How firm a foundation, ye saints of the Lord	205

I.

In the house of king David a fountain did spring	83
I love my blessed Saviour,	104
I love thee, I love thee, I love thee my love,	108
In vain my fancy strives to paint,	119
In all my Lord's appointed ways,	123
In every trouble, sharp and strong,	147
It grieves me, Lord, it grieves me sore,	182
If life's pleasures charm thee	190

J.

Jesus, at thy command,	35
Jerusalem, my happy home,	54
Jesus! and shall it evey be,	63
Jesus I love thy charming name	207

L.

Listed into the cause of sin,	33
Lift up your hearts, Immanuel's friends,	60
Lord my ransom'd soul adores thee,	102
Lord! when together here we meet,	170
Lo I come with joy to do	199
Lord, and am I yet alive	202

M.

	Page
Mercy, O thou son of David!	21
My days, my weeks, my months, my years,	106
My God was with me all the night,	127
Mortals awake, with angels join	144
My soul be on thy guard,	154

N.

Nay, I cannot let thee go,	126

O.

O Jesus, my Saviour to thee I submit,	13
O how I have long'd for the coming of God,	17
Oh give me Lord my sins to mourn	42
O when shall I see Jesus,	43
O thou, in whose presence,	45
O God my heart with love inflame,	49
O Jesus, now thy power display,	77
O Jesus, my Saviour, I know thou art mine,	78
Our souls by love together knit,	81
O may I worthy prove to see.	142
O for a breeze of heav'nly love,	159
O Zion afflicted with wave upon wave,	160
O give me Lord my sins to mourn,	165
On the brink of fury ruin,	169
O thou whose guardian care hath kept,	174
O hearken sinners we have cause	186
O why should unbelief .	204

R.

Rise my soul and stretch thy wings	113

S.

Saw ye my Saviour! &c.	7
Stop poor sinner; stop and think,	26
Sweet rivers of redeeming love,	86
Sinners hear the Saviour's call,	89
Sweet to rejoice in lively hope,	146
Stop poor sinner and look yonder;	179
Sweet muse descend and bless the shade,	181

	Page.
Soon will this mortal life be o'er,	185
See the eternal Judge descending,	197

T.

The son of man they did betray,	27
Throughout the Saviour's life we trace.	31
The voice of free grace,	36
This life's a dream, an empty show,	50
There is a land of pleasure,	52
The Lord's into his garden come.	56
There is a heav'n o'er yonder skies,	64
The wonderous love of Jesus,	66
The reason we love friendship,	67
The sacred ties of friendship,	91
There we shall reign with Jesus, &c.	93
There is a holy city,	114
The gospel's joyful sound,	128
Thou God of Jabez hear;	149
Thro' all the downward tracts of time,	150
The trump of the gospel resounds thro' the land,	167
The souls that would to Jesus press,	180
Tho' in the outward Church below.	189

V.

Vital spark of heav'nly flame.	159

W.

What happy children who follow Jesus,	79
With love and pity I look round.	110
When languor and disease invade,	145
When the fierce north wind with his airy forces,	162
When faith presents the Saviour's death,	163
Whither goest thou pilgrim stranger.	193
What various hindrances we meet,	198
When blooming youth is snatched away,	201
While on the verge of life I stand,	203
When I survey the wonderous cross,	207

Y.

	Page.
Ye children of Zion, who're aiming for glory,	5
Ye sons of war I pray draw near,	11
Ye jewels of my master,	37
Ye weary heavy laden souls,	94
Ye saints of Jesus courage take,	117
Ye humble souls approach your God,	131
Ye virgin souls arise	132
Yonder amazing sight's I see,	135
Young people all attention give,	175

APPENDIX

The lyrics in this book can be found set to tunes in these popular shape-note tunebooks:

The Southern Harmony (SoH)
The Sacred Harp, 1991 Edition (SHD)
The Southern and Western Pocket Harmonist (SWP)
The Christian Harmony, 2010 Edition (CHM)
The Shenandoah Harmony (ShH)
The Valley Pocket Harmonist (VPH)

While its possible I've missed a few tunes, this list is certainly robust enough to explore the many iterations of this poetry over the course of nearly 200 years.

A few more days on earth to spend
SoH	74	The Christian's Hope
SHD	134	The Christian's Hope
SHD	368	Stony Point
CHM	13	Traveler's Hope
CHM	327	The Christian's Hope
VPH	98	Yonder Bright Abode

Afflictions, though they seem severe
SWP	140	Returning Prodigal
VPH	7	Prodigal

All hail the pow'r of Jesus' name
SoH	299	Coronation
SHD	314	Cleburne
SHD	63	Coronation
SHD	198	Green Street
SHD	485	New Agatite
SWP	96	Coronation
CHM	129	Coronation
ShH	279	Miles' Lane

Almighty love inspire my heart
    SHH   86   Song of Moses

And will the Judge descend
    SHD   501   O'Leary

Approach my soul the mercy seat
    SoH   183   Peterborough

Attend young friends while I relate
    CHM   146T   Solemn Warning

Awak'd by Sinai's awful sound
    SWP   76   Ganges
    SHH   82   Indian Philosopher

Begone unbelief, my Saviour is near
    SWP   91   Confidence in God
    SHH   339   Begone Unbelief

Brethren we have met to worship
    SoH   103   Holy Manna
    SHD   59   Holy Manna
    CHM   323   Holy Manna

Bright scenes of glory strike my sense
    SoH   36   The Soldier's Return
    SHH   259   Mecklinburg
    SHH   318   Soldier's Return

Burst ye emerald gates and bring
    SoH   100   Elysian
    SHD   139   Elysian
    CHM   311   Elysian
    SHH   73   Exultation

Come and taste along with me
    SoH   105   Come and Taste With Me
    CHM   319   Weary Pilgrim
    VPH   222   Farabee
    VPH   298   Pilgrim's Consolation

Come saints and sinners hear me tell
    SWP   69   Heavenly Union

SHD	484	Heavenly Union
VPH	129	Union

Come ye that love the Lord indeed
SoH	289	The Narrow Way
CHM	36B	Albion
ShH	440	Arinello

Come, humble sinner, in whose breast
SoH	4b	Hanover
SoH	48b	Fairfield
SoH	84	Salvation
SHD	29a	Fairfield
SHD	94	Never Part
CHM	147	Fairfield
CHM	150	Salvation

Dark and thorny is the desert
SoH	83	Thorny Desert
SHD	545	The Pilgrim's Way
CHM	258	Thorny Desert
ShH	226	Thorny Desert

Far from my thoughts vain world be gone
SHD	280	Westford

Farewell, my dear brethren, the time is at hand
SoH	34b	Imandra New
SoH	334	The Christian's Farewell
SHD	45b	Imandra New
SWP	48	The Christian's Farewell

From whence does the union arise
SoH	39b	Union
ShH	89A	Stephens

Hail ye sighing sons of sorrow
SHD	332	Sons of Sorrow
ShH	340	A Princeton

Hark, my soul, it is the Lord
SWP	164	Lovest Thou Me
ShH	52	David's Victory

Hark! from the tombs a doleful sound
    SoH   262   Plenary
    SHD   162   Plenary
    CHM   145B   Fiducia
    CHM   146B   Bangor
    ShH   165   Doleful Sound
    ShH   168   New Durham
    ShH   200   Attention

Hark! the jubilee is sounding
    SoH   118   Jubilee
    SHD   144   Jubilee
    CHM   257   Jubilee

Hither, ye faithful, haste with songs of triumph
    SoH   136   Portuguese Hymn
    SHD   223   Portuguese Hymn
    CHM   347   Portuguese Hymn

How firm a foundation ye saints of the Lord
    SoH   69   Solicitude
    SoH   101   Sincerity
    SHD   72b   Bellevue
    SWP   43   Christian's Delight
    CHM   338a   How Firm a Foundation

How happy every child of grace
    SWP   50   Solemnity

How lost was my condition
    SoH   49   The Good Physician
    CHM   246   The Good Physician
    ShH   181   Good Physician

I love my blessed Savior
    SoH   26   The Christian
    SoH   26b   Carnsville
    SHD   109   Carnsville
    CHM   314   The Christian
    ShH   250   Carnsville

In vain my fancy strives to paint
    VPH   325   Pickard's Hymn

Jerusalem, my happy home
    SoH   198   Never Part Again
    SoH   302   Long Sought Home
    SHD   235   Long Sought Home
    CHM   159b   Long Sought Home

Jesus I love thy charming name
    CHM   133   Juniata
    SHH   217   Juniata

Lift up your heads, Immanuel's friends
    SoH   156   The Good Old Way
    SHD   213a   The Good Old Way
    SHH   326B   Good Old Way

Mercy, O thou Son of David
    SoH   23b   Charlestown
    SHD   52b   Charlestown
    SHD   56b   Villulia

My days, my weeks, my months, my years
    SoH   98   Kingwood
    SHD   266   Kingwood
    CHM   79   Kingwood

My soul be on thy guard
    SHD   372   Rockport

O for a breeze of heav'nly love
    SHD   101a   Canaan's Land

O hearken sinners we have cause
    CHM   262   Collins
    SHH   77   Collins

O how I have long'd for the coming of God
    SoH   91   Cheerful

O may I worthy prove to see
    SWP   166   The Saints' Prosperity
    CHM   121A   Prosperity

O thou in whose presence
SoH	15	Davis
ShH	18B	A Song of Texas

O when shall I see Jesus
SoH	53	Mutual Love
SoH	122	Faithful Soldier
SHD	82a	Bound for Canaan
SHD	85	The Morning Trumpet
SHD	319	Religion Is a Fortune
SHD	410b	Mutual Love
SWP	160	Oh! How Charming
CHM	244a	Mutual Love
CHM	247	Oh! How Charming
ShH	46	Conquering Soldier

O Zion afflicted with wave upon wave
ShH	93	Mosley

On the brink of fiery ruin
VPH 52	Hallelujah

Our souls by love together knit
SWP	136	The Band of Love

Rise, my soul, and stretch thy wings
SoH	47	Judgment
SoH	72b	Invocation
SHD	84	Amsterdam
SHD	131b	Invocation

Saviour visit thy plantation
SWP	106	Revival

Saw ye my Savior and God?
SoH	25	Crucifixion
ShH	443A	Crucifixion

Stop poor sinner, stop and think
VPH	119B	Warning Voice

Sweet rivers of redeeming love
SoH	166	Sweet Rivers

SHD	61	Sweet Rivers
CHM	106	Sweet Rivers
ShH	404B	Redeeming Love

The son of man they did betray
ShH	360	Mount Calvary
VPH	17	Messiah

There is a holy city
SWP	66	Holy City
SHD	101b	Holy City
ShH	102	Holy City

There is a land of pleasure
SoH	63	Land of Pleasure
ShH	35	Rose Tree

This life's a dream, an empty show
SoH	295	Glasgow
ShH	125	Islington
ShH	377	Glasgow

Vital spark of heav'nly flame
SoH	183b	Claremont
SHD	245	Claremont

What wond'rous love is this
SoH	252	Wondrous Love
SHD	159	Wondrous Love
CHM	359	Wondrous Love

When blooming youth is snatch'd away
VPH	267B	Minnehaha

When I survey the wond'rous cross
SHD	447	Wondrous Cross
CHM	105B	Hamburg

Whither go'st thou, pilgrim stranger
SWP	149	The Female Pilgrim

Ye sons of war, I pray draw near
SWP	152	Sons of War

Ye weary heavy laden souls
SHD	72a	The Weary Soul
CHM	119	Weary Souls
SʜH	322	Parrish
SʜH	203	Forster

Young people, all attention give
SoH	1	Liverpool
SoH	96	Mission
SoH	163	New Topia
SHD	37b	Liverpool
SHD	215	New Topia
SHD	204	Mission
CHM	58A	Liverpool
CHM	201	Mission